REACH FOR A
RAINBOW

REACH FOR A RAINBOW

RALPH SHOWERS

WORD BOOKS
PUBLISHER
WACO, TEXAS

A DIVISION OF
WORD, INCORPORATED

REACH FOR A RAINBOW. Copyright © 1983 by Word, Incorporated.

Library of Congress Cataloging in Publication Data
Main entry under title:

Reach for a rainbow

   1. Showers, Ralph K.   2. Baptists—United States—
Clergy—Biography.   3. Physically handicapped—United
States—Biography.   4. Rainbow Acres (Organization)
I. Title
BX6495.S495A37 1983   286'.131'0924 [B]   83-6938
ISBN 0–8499–0342–4
Printed in the United States of America
First Printing, June 1983
Second Printing, February 1984

This book is dedicated to my wife and children, who have made me the person that I am today—to Marilyn, Mark, Scott, and Mike.

Acknowledgements

To F.M.S. for making this book possible.

To Rusty Murphy for helping write the manuscript.

To Lynn Watts, Jeannette Doerksen, and Linda Markham for typing.

To Marilyn Showers for proofing.

To Dr. Cliff Barrows, Dr. Ed Dahlberg, and Dr. Bernard Ramm for reading and recommending.

To all those at Word Books for helping me publish this book.

Photo Credits

Pages 75, 77, 79—Reggie Tucker.

Page 76, top photograph—James Hammer; lower photograph—Reggie Tucker.

Page 78, top and center—Reggie Tucker; lower photograph—James Hammer.

Page 80—Showers family collection.

Page 81, top photograph—Dr. Ronald Wright; lower photograph—Reggie Tucker.

1

Today it would be real. Haul up the flag for Rainbow Acres Day. Today I would plant the barn, that first edifice on my long-dreamed-for ranch. It was to be a haven, a community for mentally retarded adults. Today was surely to be the most important day in my life. If I had realized just how important, I would have locked myself in the bathroom and never come out.

This was to be one of those days—a day marked by changes that come rarely to only a very few. Those changes would happen to me on a lonely road in the hot Arizona desert, but they would affect all those around me, and touch the lives of people I had never known. This was to be the day of my miracle—a miracle as terrifying as it was beautiful, as awful as it was joyous. But the day had not started out unusually.

Tuesday, October 23, 1973, was one of those typically perfect days that seem to exist only within the covers of *Arizona Highways* magazine. Lavender-gold cotton wisps cleared to puff-white clouds against the pale clarity of an azure morning sunrise. Craggy mesquite dotted the irrigation-fertile Verde Valley in the heart of Zane Grey's rimrock country. It was God's day. It was to be my day.

Marilyn, always the bright and vital stability of my life, was busy in the kitchen. My sons, Mark, Scott, and Michael, were banging around the house in their usual preparation-for-school calamity. I was thrilled. I, Ralph Showers, Baptist minister by trade, was about to plunge headfirst into my new life. What I didn't know was how far I would have to fall to get there.

Marilyn was depressed, which was unusual for her, but she tried to be cheerful so as not to interrupt my excitement. A teacher in the Head Start program at the Yavapai Apache Indian Reservation in Camp Verde, she regarded teaching as much a vocation as a job. She loved it, but this particular position was not her life's joy. Facing another day was not a pleasant prospect, so she struggled to share my exuberance for the morning to begin.

As for me, a whole new world was scheduled to open up this day. I was going to pick up an old grain barn Ray Smith had sold me over at the shut-down Wingfield Dairy. A forty-dollar opening kickoff for the ranch—the first actual building. A definite first step to fulfilling my dream.

All I had to do was haul that gorgeous assemblage to its assigned plot. Four months of heavy fantasy with no real foundation would at last have truth.

Marilyn had not wanted to deal with school and youngest son Michael both, so it was decided that he would go with me. We were to meet C. A. McDonald and a young man from the lumberyard over at the dairy farm after lunch. First there were chores to do, errands to run, tools to pick up and, generally, time to kill before we left. I was as excited as a schoolboy planning to play hooky.

Michael was just as excited. After all, he would actually be playing hooky. For a four-year-old, moving a barn was right up there with going fishing or watching a pro ballgame. Besides, his brothers had to go to school, and they would miss all the fun.

Mark and Scott were not thrilled about being left out. Still, they were caught up by my enthusiasm. All their lives they had heard me talking, formulating my dream. Today, at last, I was doing something about it.

Just the night before, Larry and Joy Goehner had stopped over on their way to Washington State. These were our dearest friends and partners in the ranch home dream. They were going to do some fund raising for the ranch and get in some much-needed vacation with Larry's family for the next few weeks. We wished each other good luck in our ventures, though the value I placed on that old barn escaped Larry. Nonetheless, his view was that if Ralph needed some physical manifestation that this ranch was real, some touchable sense of permanence beyond the double-wide mobile home that served as bed and office for our fledgling enterprise, so be it and good luck.

Good luck. If they only knew.

We met C. A. at the dairy and sized up the situation. What we had was a shack on stilts, a sorry-looking building that seemed to be built inside out, with smooth interior and stud-lined outside. Raised above the ground to keep the rats out of the grain, it looked like a misplaced fishing hut. We also had one truck-pulled lowboy trailer, one fork lift, and a whole lot of good intentions.

Michael was appointed supervisor, and the rest of us went to work. First we took a chain saw to the stilts, leaving the barn perched but free from the ground. Then we tried to lift the structure onto the lowboy with the forklift. We tried that maneuver every way but Thursday to no avail. Finally, in semi-desperation, we decided to hold the building firm with the lift as we backed the trailer directly under it.

After much lifting, heaving, and struggle, the proud but stubborn grain barn rested on its transport. This had been a job for Superman, but Superman had failed to show up.

Michael thought it was great fun. What did he know? What did I know? I thought I was about to lay the keystone to my dream, but what was about to happen would throw my life into a nightmare. Ignorance is bliss. I was very happy.

C. A. was no stranger to us or to hard work. His men had helped us grade and prepare our land for the mobile home only two months earlier. Spurred on by a big heart, very little cash, and a skeptical desire to see if the Showerses and Goehners could actually get this ranch for the handicapped off the ground, he had become one of our first friends in Camp Verde. Being our friend tended to mean being in for a lot of work. He was up to the challenge.

"Only one problem more that I can see." His voice rumbled aimlessly across the valley. "Now I see how high this thing is up there on the trailer, I figure we're going to hafta move a couple phone lines to get it across the valley."

Convincing my son that he didn't really want to ride atop that barn was no easy trick. He grudgingly hopped up into the cab to ride shotgun as I climbed up the cross studs to the corrugated roof of the barn. C. A. grabbed a stick—really a piece of junk wood—and drove a nail into it about three inches from the end. It formed a sort of Y with which I could fork the telephone wires that created a high fence across the roadway. There I was, a king with his scepter riding high on my mountain. I could not remember ever being happier.

"Wagons ho!" I wisecracked, and off we went with a lurch that nearly toppled me off my throne. This was the life. We were off.

A weary hawk glided in the high hot air currents and gazed questioningly down at us strange humans. It was a glorious day as the truck left the dairy and made its way along dusty roads to the turnoff that would carry us to Rainbow Acres.

The trailer hardly felt the load of the small barn perched upon it and cared less for the barn's passenger—me. Blue Arizona afternoons are hot, and the barn's metal roof amplified the discomfort as I squatted or half crawled, stradding its peak from one end to the other, carrying the low wires out of harm's way.

"Slow down," I hollered over the grind of the truck.

"Slow down," Michael echoed. His giggle testified to obvious joy at both the adventure and his unexpected reprieve from school.

"I hear ya," barked back C. A. "Any slower and I'll be pushing this thing by hand."

I wondered what C. A. stood for. Clarence, I thought, or something equally unbefitting this robust, cigar-chomping range man. He was a towering figure, huge in every respect, a sturdy pioneer type with a weather-beaten face under his beat-up Stetson. His lineage traced the history of Arizona. Tough and hard, but gentle and giving—good neighborly was the phrase.

"Hey, down there, what does C. A. stand for?"

"Nothin' much," he said. "You just call me C. A."

I had known this man only a short time, but I knew his gruff exterior belied the depth and power of his heart. He had made me feel like a long-time friend, and though he was not a jolly man, I could see that he was filled with the joy of life, of living.

"Hey, Daddy! Hey, Daddy! Here comes a low one." Michael was beside himself. Daddy was on his barn and all was right with the world.

We were having a ball. Michael bounced from window to driver's seat and back, calling up C. A.'s words and echoing mine. I was an Arizona cowboy astride my corrugated-tin–saddled horse, moving the first building to my new ranch. Nothing could go wrong.

Every now and then a wire hung so low that I couldn't hook it with my stick. I knew that phone wires carry hardly any juice, so I would reach down with my gloved hand and lift it up over the tip of the roof. Then I would place it on my stick as I turned to duck-walk it the twenty feet to the other side.

Pecan Lane was potholed from rains and tractors, so my barn horse kicked and bucked me around a bit as I moved the phone wires. On both sides of the road, the recent gully-wash had soaked the semi-arid desert irrigation ditches, and the phone poles seemed to lean in toward the drier road bed. Several feet above the wires, high-voltage power lines stretched from the same poles. I was pretty sure those things were well insulated, but the thought of seventy-two hundred volts kept me clear of them.

"They must be safe," I thought. "Why else would the power company allow them to hang so low?"

Every time a power line bent low over the trailer I would duck or twist or flatten on the sharp-angled roof to avoid it. Michael would bounce on the seat and smile at my contortions, then flash a big thumbs-up sign as the wire passed over and beyond the barn. I was pleased, glad I had brought the boy along. This was an adventure he would not soon forget—something to tell his playmates at school.

He was four years old, blue-eyed and blond like his mother, a happy child who had never really known sadness, and his eyes blazed with the innocent rapture lost to adults. His joy spilled out of the truck cab to fill the valley. He was so proud of me, and I basked in his excitement, wishing this moment would never end. I was not on top of a barn; I was on top of the world with my boy looking up at me.

We had just crossed the Verde River and had come to a small country neighborhood. Michael waved to some children playing in their new Halloween suits as I flattened down to miss an especially low power line. I reached down over the roof to grab the phone wires and haul them up to the fork on my stick.

The old nail bent and the wires dropped. I quickly grabbed them to keep them from snagging on the tin roof, then jerked them up. I was hoisting them up over my head to pass them across the barn when my back touched the sagging power line.

It was like an explosion. A bomb seemed to explode in my ears, and a searing pain shot through my body. My hands, still clutching the phone lines, jerked in horrible spasms. My brain was blasted with light, and pictures, clear as movies, flashed over my eyes.

Random thoughts from weeks or years before came glaringly clear. Forgotten memories streaked through my mind, complete with details overlooked even at their actual time. A dying man's life may flash before his eyes, but I didn't want to die.

I knew what was happening. I could feel the pain rolling over and over in my body. I could smell my flesh burning. I knew what was happening and I couldn't do anything about it. And those pictures, the sounds of today and yesterday, blared together: a snatch from a barbershop ballad I had been rehearsing a few days before; the taste of this morning's pancakes; the smell of the clean air after the rain; the three glistening rainbows; almost the complete text of a sermon I had delivered over a year before in Buena Park, California.

The pain was unlike anything I had ever known. No pain could be worse; nothing could be worse. I had heard Marilyn tell stories of our childrens' births, but this was worse. Only a few weeks earlier Michael had fractured his skull and screamed in unrelenting anguish, but this was worse.

I couldn't let go of that phone wire. I couldn't move my back off that horrible white-hot torch. I couldn't do anything.

"You must see my mother before she dies," the woman had begged. "She wants to see a minister."

I had been very busy. By the time I had arrived at the old woman's bedside, she was gone; her daughter would never quite forgive me.

Why was I thinking about this? I had no control over my brain.

"If anybody can get this church back on its feet, it's Ralph Showers." Who had said that?

Hawaii, the Baptist Church there with all my friends, flashed before my eyes. Buena Park with all of its politics. Young Larry and Joy Goehner, my very best friends, coming with me to build the ranch.

Marilyn, Mark, Scott, and Michael. Every other vision was of them or about them.

I could smell my flesh burning.

My back arched over the deadly power line. Ablaze, my eyes stared into the crystal sky, seeing only visions from the past. Seeing, for the first time in my life, no vision of the future.

Round and round, the crashing, pulsating energy thrashed through my body. *I cannot die if I keep my eyes open. I must keep my eyes open. I must keep my eyes open.* I bit down on my lip to keep my eyes open.

"Oh, God—why me? Why now? I have so much to do, so much. You can't do this to me. You can't kill me now. You can't."

Torturous, screaming, wrenching pain was about to close its death grip on all I had dreamed of. My life, just beginning, was about to end.

"Why do you want to live, Ralph?"

Who said that?

2

As I lay with my back ignited by seventy-two hundred volts, my hands searing through useless gloves, my life became a film projected on the back of my eyes. In seconds I saw what had taken me thirty-seven years to live. It all seemed so important, all those large and small moments that had brought me to this moment, to this wire.

Arizona had been the Showerses' homeland ever since I could remember. I first arrived in this land of sculptured craggy rocks and desert by way of the Good Samaritan Hospital on February 17, 1936. Hardly an event the world will long remember, the world being too much occupied with affairs of Europe to take notice of a small announcement in a Phoenix, Arizona, newspaper.

Preceded as I was by two earlier births to Byron and Naomi Showers, there was nothing noteworthy in the whole affair.

My father was up to his ears in oranges and lemons as he climbed through the years to his lofty post as manager of the Arizona-California Citrus Growers Association. Mother had her hands full enough with school children and then printer's ink and copy as a successful woman writer in those days before the feminist movement. Besides, Jim, the oldest of the Showers siblings, was already fifteen and hard at work studying to be an elementary school teacher, while my seven-year-old brother, Bob, was all over the neighborhood.

No, it was hardly an eventful day, but my family was glad for it, and they welcomed me with unending love and friendship. I was a lucky young boy, quite unaware of my own needs and unconcerned with the future.

My first six years were uneventful, at least to my own recollection. Mostly I remember being told to get off the roof, get out of the tree, and, "No, you can't fly." If there was something to go up, I would go up it. If there was a way to come back down fast, I'd take it. I was indestructible. I could do anything, and I did everything.

I met the first grade head-on and stumbled clear through to the seventh grade. There I discovered that brother Jim was to be my teacher. That didn't seem fair. He already knew too much about me.

"You've got to stop this daydreaming, Ralph, and get to work." My brother sounded more like my mother every day. "If you don't buckle down, you're going to have trouble in school from here on out."

Boy, was he right about that! But then, I never did take advice very well. My dreams always seemed more interesting.

I dreamed about everything. Life was an endless possibility. God would see me through.

I'm not sure when I first began to believe in God. Maybe always. My grandparents and my parents were regular attenders of the First Baptist Church in Phoenix. They never spoke much about faith or things like that, but they lived closely within the church's dictates. Love and kindness were all around me, and somehow God was associated with all those things.

I couldn't sit still, hold still, or be still. Everything in my life told me to keep moving. The only time I would stop would be to watch Oren Arnold writing his books. Then I would be quiet, silently watching the thoughts move across his brow. His daughter and I could sit and watch that man writing for hours, and dream of working on a newspaper or something.

With me, dreams never lasted long. Action would soon follow. Adventures were to be lived, not dreamed.

At the age of ten, creativity and compulsion took over and Rosemary Arnold and I found ourselves publishing the Pasadena Avenue News. I would write stories and she would draw cartoons (after all, the comics were the most important page in any paper). Together we would sell ads, and together we made a fortune. Mother typed the stencils, but I don't think she made a fortune. That was one of the penalties of being volunteer help.

Then there was the orange-juice stand—another fortune made. I was becoming the richest kid in postwar Phoenix.

There seemed no end to my resourcefulness in all re-gards except education. Between stirring five-pound bags of sugar into vats of squashed sour oranges and water, and dreaming of all the great events and turns my life was sure to take, I barely got out of elementary school with my multi-plication tables intact.

One of my clearest memories was that of a shiny, yellow, new (to me) Chevy convertible. My dad and I had pur-chased this street gem in our normal way. I would pay the first half and he would help with the rest. We bought it to celebrate my escaping North Phoenix High School with barely enough grades to get me what was called a proba-tionary admission to Arizona State University. This was not a flippant gesture. I had really had to bear down on the books to get my senior year grades up.

I had been class president, active in student plays and athletics, and had done everything that seemed most important for three years of school. Then came my senior year.

Church had become increasingly important to me. In my junior year at North Phoenix High, I had been elected state president of the Baptist Youth Fellowship. This kind of association made me conscious of my dream to become a minister. That dream was not totally shared by my family, but then I never did take advice very well. I did know that in order to be a minister I would have to attend college. That was probably the primary reason for my home-stretch drive for some semblance of academic standing.

Having attained admission, I fell back to my old ways. Barbershop quartet singing, strangely enough, became one of my addictions. It was never a rage among the vast majority of young people, but I never did find much fun in following the herd. Besides, I had a pretty good tenor voice.

I remember being coerced into singing in front of a school assembly. I was terrified. I had never minded speaking in public, I ran for all available offices in the school and church, but singing was a private passion and I was afraid. The audience response was tremendous. My ego soared and I could hardly be shut up from that point on.

Again, barely, I made it through ASU with scratch grades. I spent too much time dreaming, not enough time doing rote memory work. It seems I could never get as interested in what had gone before as with what was coming up. Planning for the future, I kept ignoring the present.

Always popular, always successful, my life was still a constant enigma to my friends. At parties I found myself moving to be with the ugly ducklings, the wallflowers. I called them the unlovelies. I hated to see their loneliness, their sadness. It was as if it were my responsibility to see that they were happy.

Not all unlovelies start off that way. Jim Dorsey was one of my best friends. We played football together and generally enjoyed each other's company. Both of us were well received by the "in" people at school. Then, and I'm not sure how, Jim Dorsey suffered a horrible accident. With a shotgun, he inadvertently shot and ruined his own leg.

This was my first really personal exposure to the world of the handicapped. I had a sense of powerlessness. There was no way I could help. But Jim surprised me and everybody else. He didn't let himself become an unlovely. Surrounded by a loving family, he overcame his disabled leg; he used his crutches and his spirit to find a new way to live. The knowledge that love, spirit, and an atmosphere of hope can overcome so much was a seed that took root deep in my soul. That seed was to emerge and bud through my life. I knew I wanted to help others find the hope that Jim had found—all those millions of others that no one else seemed to be able to help.

But here I was—the bud beginning to spring into a flower, about to be picked before it could really blossom.

3

I paid for all those years of daydreaming behind my school books with a desperate struggle at Arizona State. When I entered, I was, I felt, prepared for my future vocation as a minister, but I was definitely not prepared to be a college student. Still, I had to get through college if I was to get into seminary, and I had to get into seminary if I was to get behind a pulpit. I wanted to get behind that pulpit more than anything in my life.

The need to work with people, to try and help them or be a comfort to them, to do God's work, had been the driving force behind my whole life. Between my hours of effort at book learning, I took part-time jobs at churches in various capacities. I worked as a youth director and choir director, anywhere I could be of service.

Finally, with only a few units between me and graduation, my schedule was such that I would be able to handle full-time work. I needed to get down to basics, to get my life in order. A full-time church job that would allow me enough freedom to finish college was just what I needed, and just what I found.

I received an appointment as director of Christian education for the Scottsdale First Baptist Church. I was to work for the Reverend Milton Van Slyke, and under his guidance I would be able to learn my trade.

Anywhere else in the world it would have felt like summer, but it was winter in Scottsdale, Arizona. Everyone was home for the Christmas holidays. I had a new job and a very important decision to make. I had been no wallflower, and had gone out with many girls in my short life, but now I was ready to marry. It had all come down to two girls.

Marilyn Kerr, my first date from way back in second grade, was home. So was Ruthie Latham, returning for the winter break from the University of Redlands in California. I was pretty sure one of these ladies would be the future Mrs. Showers. I didn't know that they had traveled home together, along with a third young woman—Reverend Van Slyke's daughter, another Marilyn.

This was a busy time.

Everyone was convinced that Marilyn Kerr and I would marry. Having dated all through grammar school and then again in college, we seemed like such a perfect couple. But Ruthie and I had seen a lot of each other during those same years, and the long money was on her to be my bride. I planned on settling the whole thing this vacation.

Two days before Christmas we celebrated with the church's annual progressive dinner. The night began at the Van Slykes' house for the first course. For me, the first course was meeting this new Marilyn—very nice. We drove together through the progression of courses until, at last, we arrived at the church for the main course.

Part of the evening's festivities was the turning over of the keys to the church to me as a welcoming gesture. Reverend Van Slyke made a little speech and handed the keys to his daughter to give to me, which she did. I almost dropped them. She was tall and beautiful and I was about to fill my card for the evening.

Next day it was see Marilyn Kerr from 9:00 A.M. through about lunchtime; then hurry over to take Ruthie Latham horseback riding; drop Ruthie off and shag over to the Van Slykes'. I was lucky I was young; this pace could kill a man of twenty-five.

On Christmas Eve I invited Marilyn Van Slyke to a movie at the Indian Drive-In. The car was old and my heater didn't work with the ignition off. Marilyn's feet were like ice cubes. I held her feet all through the film, trying to keep them warm.

Five days of Marilyn, Ruth, and Marilyn. I was exhausted. The night before she was to return to school, Marilyn Van Slyke told me she would be driving back to California with friends.

"Hey, that's great. Who are you going with?"

"Ruthie Latham and Marilyn Kerr."

Oh, boy! I'm in trouble.

"Marilyn, there is something I have to tell you."

Out it came. Liaisons at breakfast, horseback riding for lunch and movies in the evening. I wanted everything real clean, real fast. The point was that I had fallen in love with my boss's daughter.

On the drive back, Marilyn quietly listened to the other girls tell of their holiday. About halfway to Redlands they realized they were both talking about me. Silence. Then, as an icebreaker, Ruth asked my Marilyn what she had been doing. The smile gave it away.

She had to have loved me from the start. How else could she have allowed herself to continue dating this three-timer?

Dating . . . with Marilyn in Redlands, California, and me in Scottsdale, Arizona, it wasn't easy. Sometimes we would meet in Blythe. Every so often she would go out with someone else. Not I. I was already sold. Every so often she would write to say she thought she was in love with some man from California. I would drive or bus out and talk her out of it. Once I had to fly.

That summer Marilyn was offered a chance to go back to Green Lake, Wisconsin, as a staff member at the American Baptist Conference Grounds. She decided instead to spend the summer with me, to see if we really did have something going. I went out and bought a ring.

I had always had a rule. Three times and you're out. If I asked a girl to go out and she turned me down, okay. If I asked again to no avail, well, that was okay too. If I was refused on my third attempt, that was that. Thanks very much; is your sister home? That kind of thing.

I asked Marilyn to marry me almost at once. She wasn't sure. I put the ring back in the glove compartment. Twice more I asked her in the next couple of weeks; twice more the ring ended up in the glove compartment. That was three. I asked her again; she still was not sure. Glove compartment.

I was not one to take "not sure" for an answer. Six times I took "not sure" for an answer.

My rules just didn't work with this lady. She was special. She occupied my brain like a visiting mother-in-law; I couldn't get her out. This went on for a year.

Back and forth, Arizona to California—this was getting to be a Harlequin Romance. She consulted with her friends. My life was a chess game and she and her friends were the masters.

The summer of '59 we went to a family camp in the Arizona mountains. Most people think of Arizona either as Grand Canyon or as desert with lizards and scorpions on the ground and vultures overhead, and an occasional ocotillo blossom or barrel cactus. The Arizona mountains up around Payson in the eastern part of the state are the equal for beauty to any in Oregon or Vermont: spiraling pines and fir surrounded by thick fern underbrush; brisk, clean air and trickling brooks.

Marilyn and I hiked through the woods, up to the water-pressure tank beyond the Tonto Rim Baptist Campground. She looked forward to a lovely walk; I had the glove-compartment ring stuffed into my pocket. This was to be my seventh and final attempt. No "not sure" this time.

The view from the water tank was awesome. You could see the whole world from there. The silence was splendidly interrupted by bird songs and whispering blades of grass and fern. It was idyllic until someone down at camp would turn on a faucet or flush the toilet and the tank would go into its routine.

We sat beneath a mammoth fir looking out over the rich

green and brown forest and valley. We sat right beside the water-pressure system.

"Marilyn, I know I've asked—"

Whoosh, gurgle, slosh.

"What, Ralph?"

"Nothing."

A few seconds passed. Silence and birds.

"Marilyn, I—"

Splash, burble, roar, rumble.

"What?"

"Nothing."

A few more minutes.

"Marilyn—" Burble, glub. "Will you—" Flush, blub, rumble. "For the last time, will you—" Slosh, glug, whoosh.

I was hollering. "Will you marry me!"

"Sure."

"I won't ask—"

Gurgle, rumble, blub, glug.

"Huh?"

What followed was a great deal of kissing, hugging, smiling, and love. Accompanied by a cacophonous deluge of rumble-de-glurches from the tank.

No more glove compartment.

It was 1959, a time when people asked their intended's father for permission. This father was also my boss. He was a wonderful man, but this was his daughter.

Reverend Van Slyke was up on his roof, cleaning out the mandatory Arizona evaporative cooler. My heart placed firmly in my throat, I climbed the roof to join him.

"Hey, Ralph, how are you?"

"Oh, yeah, fine. Terrific day, huh?"

"You bet."

Much shifting of weight and shuffling of feet on the roof gravel. He seemed oblivious to my discomfort.

"Uh, Milton."

"Um-hum," he kept working.

"I have to ask you a question."

"Fine." He was readjusting the screen on the cooler.

"I want to know if it's all right if I marry your daughter." I just blurted it out like a dumb fool.

"'Dyou ask her?"

"Yeah." Wow, what a dumb answer.

"She say yes?"

"Yeah."

"Well, it's all right by me. Here, take this." He handed me a dirty towel he had used to clean the oil off the mechanism and kept on working.

In one second, he handed me a towel and his daughter's hand. I was so flustered I almost missed the sparkle in his eye.

Our wedding was typical of the '50s. I had been, unfortunately, the scheming planner of so many of my friends' typical '50s weddings that I had ample cause to fear my own. I, who had been the planner of the pranks designed to make prenuptial life miserable for my friends, was about to marry.

I, who had been the instigator of the great treasure-hunt shivaree, was the potential brunt of a like happening. We had fastened a huge ball and chain to a college friend's fiancée the night before they were to be wed. Attended by some girl friends, we had left her in the desert to await rescue by her Prince Valiant. We then composed clues to her whereabouts and scattered them across Phoenix, leaving the hapless Valiant only one clue to begin with. Valiant found her, not too pleased with his adventure, and married her. Both of them would be attending our wedding. This could be dangerous.

I considered having a helicopter come in to whisk us away. I was ready to pay for it. They were out to get me. I settled on something much simpler.

Two friends, much the same height as Marilyn and I, dressed to match our wedding garb. After the ceremony, my new bride and I ducked into a nursery-school room, ostensibly to change for our honeymoon. Our friends, she veiled and he with his hand over his face, hurried out the back door under the watchful eyes of those legions of get-

Ralphers who eagerly had planned some nonsense for my immediate future. The bogus couple sped off, with everyone in hot pursuit, as Marilyn and I waited for the coast to clear.

Finally, we left, to be spotted only by Marilyn's brother and a handful of nonthreatening guests.

We fled to a hotel, known only to my brother Bob. We were safe. No one would find us; no amount of treachery would interrupt our wedding night. It was perfect.

Ten o'clock came. The phone rang. It must be Bob.

"Hello, Bob."

"This is your father-in-law. Come back here."

"No chance! How did you find us?"

"Bob told me. Listen, you've got to get right back here to the church."

"I'll kill him. Did he tell anyone else?"

"What? No, I don't think so. Now listen to me. You have to come back. I'm serious."

"I know you are. Sorry, we're busy."

"But you're not married!"

"Good grief! Marilyn, your dad says we're not married! Whaddaya mean, we're not married?"

"You didn't sign the papers."

"You must be kidding."

"No, I'm serious." And from his voice I knew he was.

"Did you do the service?"

"Of course, but the papers—?"

"Does God recognize your church?"

"Of course, but you—"

"So the only problem is the legal papers?"

"Ralph, the state of Arizona says you aren't married. Now come back here."

"Forget the papers. God says we're married. Tomorrow is time enough for the governor."

Click, buzz. I hung up and returned to my mostly wife. I would deal with the papers in the morning.

4

Marilyn had gone back to school to finish her teacher's degree the day after our honeymoon. I threw myself into my work, with a new desire to succeed today and let the future care for itself. I was a husband, and with God's blessing I would be a father. I had to succeed. But my zeal was premature.

First I had to get through seminary. In truth, I had barely made it into seminary. My grades were okay, but nothing to write home about. They were definitely not enough to get me into one of the seminaries I wanted to attend. My future, all my hopes and dreams, came smashing closed like an iron door. I had applied to three seminaries and had been turned down by three seminaries. I was locked out.

One of my professors, Dr. Engelwood (not his real name), a crusty old agnostic who had looked with a jaundiced eye toward my stated desire for ministerhood, provided the key. My whole life seemed over and I hadn't even gotten started. I couldn't let it just end like that. I didn't know where to turn or what to do, so I went to Dr. Engelwood. I don't know what made me think he could or would help, but he did. He called the dean of admissions at my seminary of first choice and talked with him. "Academics are not all-important," he had said. "Any man who wants to do God's work as much as Ralph must be allowed to try." It worked.

Marilyn finished her education courses at ASU while I

worked at the Scottsdale church and finished my studies. In August we headed to California Baptist Seminary (now American Baptist Seminary of the West) in Covina, California. I was in. And eventually I was out, a minister at last. Now what?

I was Reverend Ralph Showers, and I was going to make my living working for God. Our denomination was in a period of growth. There were places for me to go to advance myself. The church structure was like that of a giant corporation, and I was trying to become a corporate man, but it didn't work. I have never been one to take advice well when it was forced on me. In the church, as in any other large organization, there are rules, structures, power bases. I kept running into these barriers, and they were like brick walls. I had to do it my way, and there was always someone higher in authority who wouldn't let me. Budgets wouldn't allow for projects I wanted to start; room availability wasn't sufficient for programs I wanted to start. I had to succeed, but I was failing at every turn. I became angry and bitter. I resented those people who stood in my way. I believed that they were against me personally, that they didn't like me and were out to get me.

All this came to a head in Santa Clara, California, at the First Baptist Church. I was the number-two man on the staff. The number-one man, the pastor, was a professional—thorough, efficient, successful, and, I thought, totally uninterested in me or my plans. That was it. I left the ministry. I would find some other kind of work away from the bureaucracy. I turned down an offer to go to another church; I didn't even go see them. I just packed up the family, now four in number, and moved back to Scottsdale.

I couldn't find a job anywhere. Not even the Post Office was hiring. We had some savings, but they went fast.

My father-in-law would call periodically to see how the kids were. Were they being fed, were they okay, how was Marilyn doing? Each time he would phone he would men-

tion that the Valley Christian Center was looking for someone. Was I interested?

I'd been to the Center once or twice, but I didn't know
much about it. Was there a professional minister in charge?
Yes! No thanks; I'm through with that.

Need changes minds. One day I looked at my family and
saw the effects of weeks of growing poverty. I stuck my
pride in my pocket and went to the Christian Center to ask
about the job. The kitchen cupboard was getting bare.

The Valley Christian Center was a bleak structure standing in the middle of a down-and-out area. This was a time of
civil unrest and racial tension, marked across the country by
protests and assassinations, and represented in the greater
Phoenix area by street gangs and disillusioned young people with nowhere to go and nothing to do. The Center
hoped to provide a refuge to these unhappy children as
well as a place for the joining of Christian ideals.

I met with the man who was to be my boss. I was to be the
men's and boys' worker at the Center, forty-two hundred
dollars a year and a house. I needed the job.

"What am I supposed to do?" I asked the middle-aged
black man I sat across from.

Amos Dudley looked back at me and said, "Play Ping-
Pong and pool."

"Play pool?"

"Yes, at night."

"You're kidding! You mean I get paid for that?"

"Yes." He smiled at me, and then added in all serious-
ness, "You're supposed to get to know the kids, the older
folks and the children. Evangelize them. You know, bring
God to them."

My problem wasn't with God, kids or Ping-Pong, it was
with professionals. "I'll take the job," I said eagerly. "When
do I start?"

"Tomorrow night," he said and handed me a set of keys.

I flew home and grabbed Marilyn to show her the house

that was to be our home. In my excitement I had forgotten to look at it myself before showing Marilyn. What we mostly saw were weeds. They stretched way above our heads, leaving only a partial view of this rundown old bungalow. We sat down and laughed and cried. We had a home. Now all we had to do was dig through to it and rebuild it. It was a mess, but I had a job, and the children would not be hungry.

I opened the doors of the Center the next night and prepared myself to meet the world. The first person I was to meet was a man I will call Jesus Ortega, a 6' 2", huge Mexican street tough with a knife scar that crossed his face below his eyes.

"What's yer name?"

I told him my name was Mister Showers. I wasn't ready to use "Reverend" yet.

"Well, 'Mister' Showers, I rob houses. Does Jesus love me?" I have never heard the Name used so mockingly.

"Yes!"

"Fine," he said, and pushed past me to the pool table.

Things went on like this for weeks. Most of the Center's visitors were polite, or at least noncommittal, but every day Jesus Ortega would bring in his snotty question. "I just beat up my wife. Does Jesus love me?" Every day I would tell him yes and every day he would shove me aside as he moved to the pool table.

Finally I couldn't take it anymore. Ortega came in and I tossed some boxing gloves at him. "You and I have some things to straighten out," I said, pointing to the next room. With a neutral man in tow we headed off to the room to get things straight. Thirty seconds later I lay flat on my back, out cold. Nobody told me Ortega had been the local Golden Gloves champ. Plus that, he had me by fifty pounds and at least five inches. All I had done was to make my life more difficult and him more snotty. I had made him boss of the Center, and he took full advantage.

Several days later he was hitting the pool balls so hard they were flying all over the room. People were leaving, those not afraid to come in the first place. Never one to learn a bad lesson well, I told him to get out. If he couldn't act like an adult, he should leave until he grew up.

He pulled a knife and came at me. Now I had done it. I was ready to fold up. What should I do? I swung out my hand with all my strength and hit his wrist. The knife skittered across the floor. We both flew after it, and I stood up first with the weapon in my hand.

I looked up into his eyes and realized that he was as scared as I. Slowly, never leaving his gaze, I walked to the wall, set the blade at an angle against the edge of the floor and wall, and broke it with my foot. I picked up the pieces and tossed them in the garbage.

"Now," I said, "You get out of here and don't come back until you can behave like a decent human being."

He left and I went into the back room to shiver for the next two hours.

Early on in this job I had given myself the goal of trying to deal with the street gangs. There were already several small, well-organized groups with a lot of energy and a need to feel important. I had to find a way to use that energy and satisfy their sense of value. I decided to turn gangs into teams—basketball teams.

I went to court for a couple of the nearer gangs and had the judge put them in my care. I brought them back to the Center and put uniforms on them. They were used to wearing their "colors," their street identification that let the world know they were a group, so the change was appropriate. They were used to working together closely for the protection of their lives, now they could use that closeness creatively.

After the scene with Ortega, word got around that I was all right. I hadn't called the police and I had stood up to one of the meanest. The gangs began to trust me. I told them I would find them games, and good courts. Our court, at best, was bad. With the help of the Phoenix YMCAs I was able to keep my word. Soon whole gangs were coming to me and taking out their aggressions on the courts instead of the streets.

Jesus Ortega was never a part of this. He came by only occasionally after the knife incident, just to show I hadn't really beaten him. He was still rude and obscene, but never stayed long enough to cause trouble.

One night his mother called me at home. Jesus was in the hospital with multiple stab wounds. He had been stabbed seven times in the chest by his brother who had caught him in bed with the brother's wife. He was in a coma; he was going to die; would I come?

You bet I would come. At last I would be rid of him and I would get points for having been at his side. What a fitting way for him to go. Everyone in the streets would be talking about it, and about how I had been so good as to go to his side. It was like a movie and I was Pat O'Brien to his James Cagney. Perfect.

I met his mother at the hospital. She was in the emergency room next to his cold table. He was unconscious. I tried to comfort her, using all the standard Christian jargon. And then Jesus Ortega came to.

He rolled stiffly over to his side and looked at me for a long second. His voice was soft and filled with pain as he asked me, "Now, Mr. Showers, does Jesus love me now?"

That was the point in my life where everything else became a façade. Even my ministry to that point was a façade. I had lived halfway. I had not served God or man; I had served Ralph. I looked down into those slowly glassing eyes and whispered, "You bet He does." At last I believed it.

I walked out of the hospital into the brisk night and stood in the open air. As I drove home, I told God that He could have anything He wanted. "From now on it's all Yours, God. I'll do it Your way."

This was the first turning point in my life. From this point on everything seemed to turn to gold. Valley Christian Center began to flourish. My ministry, and my ability to accept my ministry, blossomed. Even through pitfalls and traps that lay ahead of me, I was now able to move through my life with a knowledge I had always had, but never really believed. Jesus loved me. If Jesus loved Jesus Ortega, and He did, Jesus loved me.

And more than that, I had a destiny. I did not know what it was, but I knew it was there. Jesus Ortega had shown me my life. What was I going to do with it?

5

Was I like Job, being put to the test for my faith, or like Moses, being trained for some future task? My life was a constant stream of starting and stopping, of new experiences that tried my soul or strained my skill. Always I was facing new adversaries, new professionals who cared more, I thought, for coffers than converts. Always I had the support of Marilyn and my children; but, always, I had more life to live, more tests to face, more lessons to learn.

From Valley Christian Center I was called to pastor a church in Ewa Beach, Hawaii, a little church that was dying. I told them of my experience with young Jesus Ortega, and my knowledge that God loved us and would help us. Thirteen people joined hands with me and agreed to give the Lord a year. If He wanted this church to live, He would let it live.

Miracles were about to enter my life. Little everyday occurrences were beginning to join with coincidences and slightly improbable circumstances to become momentous occasions. A little church at the edge of a Navy base, declining into death for years, grew almost overnight to a thriving body of well over six hundred souls. Like Lazarus, this church had been buried, only to rise again to bask in the glory of God.

Ewa Beach was a little sugar-cane town of barely two thousand people, a couple of stores, an eating place, a gas station, and a bowling alley. Half the people were locals—a mixture of Hawaiian, Japanese, Chinese—and the other half were military. Of these two thousand, almost half were kids or young people with nothing to do and almost nowhere to go. There were no parks, no recreational facilities, no nothing—only the bowling alley that stood across from the church.

The bowling alley decided to open up a bar. That would have closed down the only available entertainment for the kids. I was mad. Talking to, even yelling at, the proprietors had no effect. There was money in liquor and very little in kids. This could not be allowed to happen, but I had no idea what to do.

The bowling alley was the constant conversation around the church and among our new friends. One of these friends was an attorney for the military. He was the one who showed me the light.

"You're dealing with the liquor commission here, Ralph, a very political group. You know there's rottenness everywhere. There is something rotten stuck in almost everything, especially politics."

Those were true words, but still no real help. How could that make any difference?

"I don't know how to stop this bowling alley thing," he said. "But can I make a suggestion?"

"Anything!"

"Well, why don't you go down to the liquor commission office and look through their files? All their paperwork has to be open to the public, so they have to show it to you. Nobody ever does that. You'll scare 'em to death."

"But what am I looking for?"

"Nothing; it doesn't matter. You wouldn't understand any of what you saw anyway. But they don't know that." He had a wicked sparkle in his eye. I think he had wanted to do this very thing himself. "You just walk in there like you know what you're doing and go 'hmm' every so often."

Well, I loved it. I didn't know if it would get any results, but it would certainly be worth doing, if only out of contrariness. So I went down there, looked through reams of meaningless stuff and "oh'd" and "ah'd" a lot.

People started asking me who I was and what I was looking for. I told them I was Reverend Showers from Ewa Beach and I was concerned about this bowling alley liquor license thing. Could they help? No, I was just looking, thank you. Then I drove back home.

The next morning I received a phone call from the mayor. Would I come by for a talk? I'd be glad to. I was there in thirty minutes.

He asked what my problem was, so I told him about all those kids with no place to go. Couldn't he give us a break for a few years, until Ewa Beach could get back on its feet? Besides, there were plenty of bars around.

What followed was him explaining a lot of legal mishmosh that made less sense than the papers I had read the day before, stuff about footage from church property and things like that. Then he asked what I had learned at the liquor commission office. I had never told him I had gone there.

"Oh," I said with a firm look, "some very interesting things, but I haven't got it all together yet." This was fun.

The mayor made some telephone calls and there seemed to be some question concerning the liquor license that had been issued.

"What can I do to help you?" The man looked straight across his desk at me.

"I don't want that bar and I do want a nice new park with facilities." I was victorious. We got both. The church swelled to even higher numbers. We weren't dying; we were alive.

In fact, the church was doing so well, especially the young people, that we decided to hire a youth pastor for the summer. The kids raised the money and charged me to go to the California Baptist Seminary to bring back the very best.

I wrote to the Seminary to tell them I was coming. I told them what I wanted and felt sure I would get it. Anyone who doesn't want to come to Hawaii for the summer is out of his nut. In barely enough time for the postman to turn around, I got a reply from one of the professors.

What he said, roughly, was that he knew what we wanted, felt we deserved it, was sure we could get it, but he had a young student there that he would rather send. He's kind of mixed up inside, the letter said—he doesn't know what he wants to do. I think he ought to be with you. Will you take him?

What could I say? Sure! So I flew to California to see this pig in a poke, Larry Goehner.

Long hair down over his shoulders, flighty, rebellious, he was the epitome of what was going on those days—the whole bag. I sat down with him and I liked him.

"Do you want the job?" I asked.

"Yeah, I guess so."

"You're going to have to cut your hair. Most of our church is made up of military. Do you understand?"

"Yeah."

So many of these kids were running off to Canada, marching with picket signs, fighting so hard against what seemed to them so useless a war, so corrupt a society. All I needed to do was bring back this representative of all those things my church members feared. They'd kill me—after they got through with him. But I knew he was right for us, and we for him.

Everyone in the church was there to meet him when he finally arrived to go to work. He exited his plane in neat shoulder-length hair. He was ready to work the summer. What he did was work the summer, the winter, and clear around the calendar for a year and a half. Then he went home to finish seminary. That lasted two weeks. He phoned me; could he come back? He did and stayed through my last year at Ewa Beach.

Larry Goehner joined my family. He was my best friend and my oldest son. And he was restless. He was ready to go out of his mind and take Marilyn and me with him. Then he met Joy.

He was directing the choir and Joy came to join. He fell in

love before she got to her place. He fell faster than anything I've ever seen, faster than I fell for Marilyn. I tried to hold him back, to say whoa, wait a minute. The sucker fell anyway and I was too proud and happy to speak. I loved them both.

Finally time came for me to leave Ewa Beach. I had been there when I was needed, and now it was time for someone else to take over. I accepted a position at Buena Park, California, and bid Larry, Joy, and my friends goodby. Marilyn, Mark, Scott, and little Michael joined me in our sorrow at leaving this paradise of love and friendship.

Larry resigned shortly before I left. He tried selling insurance, but with little success. Still unsure of where his life was to lead him, he returned to finish seminary. Something was working on him, though, compelling him to keep close to me—maybe because of our talks, about almost everything, maybe because of the dream I had shared with him about a ranch home for handicapped people.

Whatever the reason, he showed up on our doorstep a few months later, a seminarian with no place to go. He came in, and we talked for a while about nothing much and then went for a walk around our neighborhood. We saw an apartment for rent and he took it. Larry and Joy were back, with family, and all was okay.

I used a little influence to get him a part-time job at the church as the youth coordinator. He needed a little more money, so he took a job as night clerk for the Magic Carpet Motel across from Disneyland. Between his studies and work and my work we were both busy, but we spent whatever spare time we had with each other. Very different people, from very different backgrounds, we were more alike than brothers. Our families became one family. Together we would find our destinies. Both of us knew there was something we had to do and were meant to do, but we didn't know what or where.

6

The incident with Jesus Ortega had given me strength in my faith. The wonderful experience at Ewa Beach had given me faith in myself and my ministry. Meeting and knowing the Goehners had given me the chance to reopen my heart to a long-held dream. I came to Buena Park with a sense of excitement, of purpose and determination. I met a brick wall of bureaucracy and frustration.

When we came to Buena Park the church was broke; we set out to try to make it well. The congregation was marvelous. They gathered around our efforts with love and support so that by the end of that year we had more than quadrupled what was in the coffers. Politics, however, reigned supreme in the upper regions of the laity. We had hoped to use this new wealth to develop new programs for the membership and the community. My hopes were shattered by my old enemy, the professional church, the coffers-over-converts people.

I knew I couldn't get everything I wanted right off, but I had been elated that there would at least be enough money to get the church going. The trustees' meeting was scheduled for the Monday after the Sunday that our pledge goal had been reached. I bought coffee and donuts for the meeting and generally felt like having a party. I was so happy I was singing, but nobody showed up.

I couldn't understand. I waited for hours before I learned that they were all meeting at the treasurer's house,

and I hadn't been invited. Then I grew angry, furious. I
went to the house to which I was not invited and stormed in.
"Why aren't we having the meeting where we're supposed
to have it?"

"Because we don't want to."

I couldn't believe it. I tried to calm myself. I was a big boy
now. This was not another clod fight with the kids from the
other neighborhood.

"Okay, let's look at the budget."

They showed it to me, already completed, exactly like the
budget from the year before, not a penny more.

"Let's talk about the new money and what we're going to
do for the Lord."

"You don't believe in that bull, do you?"

I got up and went home to Marilyn. We just shivered and
cried.

All during this year, I had shared my dream of the ranch
with Larry, Joy, and Marilyn. It seemed a nice dream and
we all soon shared it, but it was, of course, a dream.

That last comment from the man at the trustees' meeting
became the momentum to move.

Of course I believed in "that bull" of using the new money to do something for the Lord. Because I did, I found
myself again at a turning point. "Marilyn, now is the time to
build the ranch. Let's go. Let's go this weekend to look for
land."

God had wanted me to move on. I had done the best I
could for this church. Now I had another task. Marilyn and
I stuffed bags and boys into the car and headed off to
Wickenburg, Arizona. We had no thought of our lack of
funds, just a vision of land my family owned in Wickenburg. Perhaps that would be the place to begin a dream.

It was late Friday night, and we realized how broke we
were in terms of cash and no banks were open. We decided
to drive further north to my parents' cabin in Oak Creek. I
knew where they hid the key, and it was free.

Since we were in the area and it wasn't too late, I phoned

old friends in a tiny town south of Oak Creek. I just wanted
to talk to someone about something other than those gen-
tlemen at the trustees' meeting. Shirley Brown and his wife,
Charlotte, were the owners of the Camp Verde pharmacy,
special people who never seemed put off by my dreams of
future glory. I told them what Marilyn and I had planned
and they begged us to look around the Camp Verde area, so
they could help.

We never got to Wickenburg.

On the way back to California I asked Marilyn if she
thought the Goehners would want to join us, since they had
listened in and shared so much of my idle wishes. Larry was
looking around for a church of his own at that time. Maybe
he would settle for a fantasy.

We had never really told them why we stormed out so fast
or what we were going to do. Understandably worried then,
Larry and Joy came over shortly after we returned. We
shared the unpleasantness at the treasurer's meeting and
they shared something they had been talking about that
day. Larry didn't really want to start in a new church; he
really wanted to work with Ralph to start that ranch we had
talked about. Was I still interested? I'm not sure where the
string of miracles began, but this was another of those just-
too-much-to-be-coincidences that were to follow one after
the next.

Larry and I drove back out to Camp Verde the next
weekend to buy a house with some land. We found what we
wanted almost immediately and headed straight to the savings and loan institution. We had $145 between us, clutched
tight in our pockets. We were going to start.

"Do you have any collateral?"

"What's that?"

The woman at the bank was another of those disappoint-
ments that were to follow one after the other.

"Like houses, or land, or something." This was not a fun
person.

Larry said some smart remark that did not go over very

well and I followed by offering to sell our wives, which fell even flatter.

Across the loan papers for $60,000 and all our hopes, the woman scrawled the single most offensive four-letter word I had ever seen: VOID.

"How did you expect me to give you this loan without any collateral or anything?"

"God wants us to build a ranch."

"Well, then, ask God for the money."

This was definitely not a fun person.

Despondent, we walked over to the pharmacy to spill our tale of woe to the Browns.

They had a little chunk of land northwest of the town they didn't mind selling if it would do.

Now these were fun people.

In a few hours we were standing on a little hill looking down at wild flowers. Ten acres of high desert without a tree to the parcel.

"If you put five thousand dollars down," the Browns said, "we'll sell you the ten acres for twenty thousand dollars with no interest or principal for the first year."

Ignoring the fact that we didn't have five thousand dollars, we pumped their hands in glee and headed home. Reality struck about Blythe, California. We gulped and decided each would try to raise half.

Once home, we hit on everything and everybody. No insurance policy was safe. By the end of the week we had enough; by the end of the next week we had a piece of paper. Now all we needed were jobs somewhere nearer the land than an eight-hour drive.

The *Verde View*, a two-page local with three help-wanted ads, took care of Marilyn. She would be a preschool teacher for the Head Start program. Now what about the rest of us? Two Baptist ministers—one not too popular with his current church trustees, and the other brand new to the profession—were a tough package to sell. Or so we thought.

Out of the blue Dr. Jeffords from Phoenix phoned.

"I hear you might be moving to Arizona."

How had he heard that?

"There is an American Baptist Indian Mission just off the Middle Verde Road in Camp Verde. Would Larry like to work there?"

We had bought ten acres across the street from that mission and I had no idea it even existed.

"Yes!"

"How would you like to be interim pastor for Hope Baptist Church in Phoenix?"

I just looked up in the air and said, "This is too much, Lord, too much."

"Pardon me?"

"Never mind, Dr. Jeffords. Yes, thank you very much."

Now, leaving a Baptist ministry is one of the best-kept secrets in Christendom. The Methodists and Presbyterians move, but Baptists sneak. I had not told anyone I planned to leave the Buena Park church, and neither had any of the others. The Browns weren't even American Baptists and I was sure the bank lady had completely forgotten us.

I am not one to question that which is set before me. We headed back to Arizona to set up shop.

The next banker was a breeze. We were well-employed land barons. We got a loan and bought a double-wide mobile home to set on the hill where we had stood a couple of weeks earlier.

C. A. McDonald leveled the ground for us. He was a good man and offered to help us if we needed it down the road.

So now, here we were with a nice new mobile home, on a nice new plot of desert, without any water or electricity. It was summer 1973, and the pioneer spirit that filled us did not quite include walking to town to lug back water.

"How do we get water?"

Larry shrugged and said he knew of only three places—from the sky, from the ground, and from town. This was Arizona's high desert, so from the sky was definitely out. Water from the town would cost three times a fortune and the bankers were not that much in love with us. So it had to be from the ground.

"My uncle is a witcher," Larry suggested tentatively.

"What's a witcher?"

"You know—with a divining rod. He finds water."

I told Larry that if I were going to trust to luck I'd rather do it through God than a witcher. With that I picked up a small white pebble and knelt down. Larry joined me as I prayed over that tiny stone and I tossed it over my shoulder.

I was beginning to take miracles rather for granted at this point. It was kind of a paranoid faith—like, okay God, what's the next obstacle I'm going to have to trust you to overcome?

The rock had landed on top of a hill.

"Not very likely," said Larry. "Better throw it again."

"Why?"

"Well, this is hardly scientific."

"My rock is as scientific as your witcher."

"It ought to be on lower ground."

"Did we pray? Did we throw the rock? Did the rock land? We'll dig here!"

We dug and hit one of the greatest wells in the entire valley. So much for unscientific rocks.

A man from town, Billy Port Parker, came in and put in our leach line and septic tank. He was another of those early acquaintances from town who stayed long enough to hear about our dream. Like C. A. McDonald, he offered his help if we ever needed it.

We had a home. Now to build a ranch. We wanted to call it Rainbow Ranch, in honor of the many rainbows Larry and I had seen hovering over our dream land, but the name was already taken by another ranch somewhere in Arizona, so we filed our papers as Rainbow Acres. After all, we had a whole ten of them. Now for a building, perhaps a barn.

7

Thirty-seven young years old, I was, I feared, about to leave this life. Wracking echoes of former lives beat at my brain. I had come this far. Larry, Joy, their son, Marilyn, my boys, and I had left everything and trekked to these vast, untamed lands to build a ranch for handicapped people. With $145, an improbable dream, a dauntless sense of purpose and total lack of sense, we had left the Buena Park congregation and tossed our fleece before the Lord.

Why in God's name am I hanging here? I was furious.
If I close my eyes, I'll die. I can't feel my hands.
My brain was pounding, jarring, careening from one thought to the next.
"Ralph, you've got to stop daydreaming."
"Your grades aren't good enough for college."
"Boy, are you stuck up."
"Ralph, stop running in church."
"Get off the banister."
"Get out of that tree, you'll kill yourself."
"Ralph, why do you want to live?"
Suddenly everything was still. There was no more pain, no noise. I could no longer smell the putrid stench of my flesh. The memories stopped, the glare faded. My eyes were still open, but they no longer saw the sky.

47

"Ralph, why do you want to live?"

A peace came to me, a serenity. I don't know what God looks like, but I say it was Him.

"Why do I want to live!" I was screaming at the top of my voice. "How can You allow me to die? I'm too young! I haven't even begun yet. I have to see my boys grow up. I have to see the ranch come true. Marilyn and I have to be able to live our lives together. I have to live! You have to let me live!"

Anger was rushing through my body at seventy-two hundred volts a second. How dare I be made to die. I dreamed of doing something great for God and my fellow men. I would not die! I would not close my eyes and go to sleep. I didn't care how much it hurt. I was not going to leave yet.

The vision, clear and peaceful in my sight, seemed unmoved, impassive. Could He hear me? Didn't He know what I was saying?

I knew perfectly well that this was God. I could not see Him, really. There was just this blurred form in the picture frame, but I knew it was God.

And why the picture frame?

I had never seen a picture of God like that. Nobody has ever seen a picture of God. I had seen likenesses of Jesus all my life—but I was sure this was God himself. Why the picture frame—or was it a window?

It couldn't be a hallucination. All the other pictures and memories were hallucinations. I could still feel the blistering pain of the wire; I could smell the awful smell; I could hear the screaming children who watched me lurch and tremble to the electricity. But all that was gone.

"Okay, Ralph."

Okay? God had said "okay" to me. This was too ludicrous.

Then it started again, the pain and all the rest.

"Get me off of here!" I yelled to the world. "Please get me off of here!"

And what had happened? I had fallen back against a high-power line while standing atop a barn in the middle of the road. Mike was the first to see the sparks and hear the explosion. C. A. threw on the brakes and pulled the petrified child from the cab.

"Is he dead? Is he dead—is my Daddy dead?" Michael was panicking. "Please, somebody, help Daddy!"

Children and adults from the small cluster of houses ran in horrified amazement to see what was happening. Witches' and devils' masks were discarded and terrified little eyes glued themselves to my situation. The spectacle was hypnotic. No one wanted to look, but no one could turn away.

Down the road about a mile, a dump truck traveled an unaccustomed route, having just emptied a load of gravel for a septic tank. In the cab, Billy Port Parker was oblivious to what lay ahead. This was the same Billy Port Parker who had just helped Marilyn and me put in our septic tank a few weeks earlier—the same Billy Port Parker who, like C. A., had become one of our first good friends in the valley.

He turned to Pecan Lane.

Not far down the road, Marilyn had just finished shopping after school and was heading home. Her normal path would have taken her past the accident. She thought about trying to catch up with us, but figured she would never be able to get around that big rambling barn. She changed her mind and took a different street home. This was one of God's blessings.

The huge dump truck, the only possible vehicle in a little town like Camp Verde that could have been of any help, came rambling down Pecan Lane.

Seconds were passing. My thick work gloves were already so much cinder, my hands were next.

Billy saw what was happening. He saw his new friend burning to death way up on that barn. With no thought for his own safety, he swung the giant truck around and slammed in the lever to raise the bed.

"Get me off of here! Please! Somebody get me off of here!" I screamed.

"We're coming, Ralph. Just a second, we're coming."

Billy was desperately climbing up the dump bed. He reached out to grab me.

"Don't touch him! He'll kill you," came a cry from the crowd of stricken spectators.

"Don't be a fool."

Just then the power shut off—an automatic mechanism that breaks the circuit after two minutes of malfunction.

Billy didn't know the power was off, he just knew that I was there and he had to get me down. He grabbed my boots and yanked me down from behind. I fell to my face on the roof. The power came back on.

The power going off was God's blessing; the dump truck was God's blessing; Billy Port was God's blessing. God had said, "Okay, Ralph." I was going to live.

All I was aware of was the pain and the strange realization that a hand had grabbed my foot and pulled me off the wire. A hand that would have surely been riveted to my own body and burned to death along with its owner and me, had the power stayed on a second longer.

One quick pull and I was off the wire. I don't remember letting go of the phone lines, but I was on my face atop the peak of the slope-roofed barn.

Now there was more pain, but this was different—an incurable ache and throb over my whole body. My eyes, still wide open, stared ahead at my sprawled arms and hands. They were charcoal, twisted black claws wrapped in scorched gloves. My back pulsated.

I couldn't believe it. I was lying atop that sharp-peaked roof. The irony was unbelievable—I was sure I would roll off the thing and crash eighteen feet to my death.

"Get me off of here or I'll die."

This was too much. *Why me, Lord?* I was almost more scared now than I had been before.

The bodies of strangers clambered up the sides of the barn to gently lift me from my perch.

Hands were grabbing at me. Each finger was a knife cutting into my body. They lifted me down into the dump bed. My eyes bulged wide open. I was going to live. I felt the thrill all through me. It was as though I had conquered a world. It was the greatest thing I'd ever felt.

An ambulance had been summoned. Again, in a town of strangers, one of our few friends was the driver. Shirley Brown, who had sold us our land and had encouraged our building in the Verde Valley, ran to the vehicle, unaware of who was to be his passenger. The battery was dead. Frantic minutes of labor to get the ambulance moving were in vain. It was not going to turn over.

Another ambulance was called from Rimrock, seven miles away. It raced through the waning afternoon to reach me.

I lay face down in the dump bed, my arms and back a smoldering ruin. God had spared my life, but there was no bargain about easing my anguish.

"Call Marilyn; tell her what's happened." Now I was barking out orders like a drill sergeant. Why God spared an ego like mine is unfathomable.

"Somebody take care of Michael. Take him away from here." I supposed nobody else was thinking at the time, but then my brain was still working at a lifetime a minute.

"We got him, sir. Keep calm. You'll be fine."

It was a woman's voice. She was feeding me an ice cube to clear my parched throat. A medical technician, she knew better than to give me water, but that ice cube kept me alive.

I knew they were taking care of Michael; I knew they would call Marilyn. I knew I was going to live.

Ray Smith, the man who had sold me the barn, happened by. After helping me down from the barn, he sped to my house for Marilyn. He told her there had been an accident but that I was all right. He did not tell her how serious, but he eased her fears. That was another of God's blessings. He had been a stranger less than a week before.

I felt a sharp pain as I was being placed on a stretcher and then into an ambulance.

"Look at his back."

"Ohh—how awful."

Voices—pitying, sorrowful. I hated that. I knew they were being kind, but I heard the pity and I hated it. Pity was an emotion I had often had for others, but I had never felt it directed at me. *My God, what must I look like?* My hands were curled black embers. *My back must look like burned meat.* I could not stand their pity. *Please save me from this pity.*

I would not let myself curse. I wanted to, but I would not let myself. Moan, groan, cry in pain, yes! But I would not curse. I had to be an example. I was a minister of God and there were people watching me. I would not let them down.

Gently the ambulance drivers lifted me from the dump bed to the stretcher. The jarring sting of unexpected contact jolted me from my reverie. The memories that had insulated me from my agony were gone. Only the pain was there. Carefully they shoved me into the ambulance. The pain was too great. I couldn't stand it.

The siren shrilled its demand for clearance. I was on my way to the hospital.

Time passed—I'm not sure how long. It must have been eight or nine at night when Marilyn finally came.

I had asked the nurses to cover my burns. Marilyn was not comfortable in hospitals, and I was afraid the sight of my back and arms would upset her. A hastily placed covering concealed my disfigurement.

As she entered, her concern was obvious. No one, however, had told her of the extent of my damage. She was calm and loving.

The sheet fell away from my hands. She was shocked, but strong. I thanked God. Both of my hands lay burned and bone-bare before her. My fingers were twisted like ravaged claws; my arms were the tips of discarded match sticks. She could not see my back, but she could imagine. I was terrified that Marilyn would run from me in disgust. She did not show one sign of pity. She told me she loved me and we would get through this thing together. Dear God, I love Marilyn.

My marriage was real, and so was my pain. The worst was over, I thought. I was wrong. The pain had only just begun.

I passed out.

God had said "okay," but He had not said "okay" to what. I was alive; at least I knew that much.

I had hung on the wire for less than two minutes. This, and much more, they told me later. Now I slept and dreamed of Rainbow Acres.

8

I had been in hospitals before. I remembered the blandly sterile attempt to be brightly cheerful, the hard thin beds made harder by stretched sheets tucked in at all sides. This room was the same, with a wood-grained metal night table with plastic utensils and goose-neck lamp—a cocooned world surrounded by a faded yellow shower curtain.

I was not yet awake enough to recognize the over-all body throb that culminated in searing pain at the end of my arms. My hearing was blunted by the silent pounding of my own heart. I could not hear the hush of the hospital. It was night, and the whole world was asleep except for one Ralph Showers.

Slowly lifting my head, I tried to see my hands. A quick glimpse of bandages was all I managed before the pain hit and knocked me out. I didn't dream.

I was in the intensive care unit at the hospital in Cottonwood. Lying on my belly so as not to put pressure on my back, I.V. tubes pushed their fluids into my veins, keeping me alive, trying to keep the blood from coagulating, trying to prevent the unpreventable—gangrene.

Clear memory returned to me with the ride to Phoenix. Cottonwood was not equipped to handle severe burn cases, so I was loaded onto an ambulance bound for Maricopa County Hospital. My eyes opened as the ambulance doors slammed closed.

"Well, you're looking better." It was the driver.

"Huh?" I'm a man of few words.

"You don't remember me? Of course not. Quite a mix-up with your boy back there."

"Huh?"

He had a deep, loving chuckle that I would come to admire in the future. At this moment, though, I had no idea what he was talking about.

"I'm John Jenkins, Reverend John Jenkins. I helped take care of your son back at the accident."

"Do I know you?" My end of this conversation was going nowhere.

"No, I'm just another one of the faces that were staring at you in that dump truck. One of the ladies had sent your boy off with her kids. Nice lady. Didn't really know what to do with him after, though. I picked the boy up and took him with me."

"Thanks."

There was that chuckle again.

"Well, I don't know. I stirred up a bit of a hornets' nest, you know. Your wife was told that the child was at Mrs. Emory's place, so she ran over there and he was gone. By then, I had dropped him off at your place. What a mess, but it all worked out. Your wife is a fine lady."

I loved this man.

I was beginning to get up some wind, and we talked the whole way to Phoenix. About the ranch, about my family, about everything but the accident. Two hours. The beginning of a lifetime.

Phoenix is sprawled out all over everywhere. From my bed in the back of the ambulance I could see the tops of signs, trucks, buildings. I could feel John's stops and starts, moves and bends as he hurried me through the freeways and streets. Other than the pain, which was still unbearable, it was a pleasant trip. But it was nothing to prepare me for what lay ahead just outside the hospital!

My time as interim pastor for Hope Baptist there in

Phoenix had been wonderful. The parishioners were beautiful, and the staff was absolutely free-spirited. Talking to John as we drove south, I recounted the tale of the day I had become King of the West.

The American Baptist home office had wanted to hang pictures of all the Baptist churches in the area. Please send a 5 x 7 picture, they had asked. I only had an 8 x 10, which I sent.

A note came back that said, "Please send a 5 x 7. We can't have Hope Baptist having the only 8 x 10 on the wall."

I took the returned photo and cut it up, moved the pieces around and repasted it as a 5 x 7. My secretary and some of the other church workers helped me in this mischief. We then mailed it back to the home office together with a book-length letter. We had said that they must surely accept this photo, as the King of the West was planning a visit to review the picture wall.

On the day and time specified in the letter (we had parked a block away and waited in order to be precisely punctual), armed with a recording of a boisterous Sousa march, we pulled up in front of the office. Music blasting, the chairman of my board of deacons hopped from the driver's seat and humbly hurried to open the rear door, revealing me, the King of the West. Bedecked in drum major's cap and choir robe, I strode regally into the American Baptist Convention office upon an unrolling red aisle carpet.

Every office door had opened, and every worker stood watching.

Arching to my full 5' 8", I marched through the hallowed halls to the wall. There I sought and found the picture, a jigsaw puzzle of Hope Baptist. Nodding appreciatively, I turned and made a royal exit. Just as I was leaving, a secretary met me at the door and presented me with a bouquet of withered flowers.

No one cracked a smile. All was perfectly in accord with the arrival and passage of royalty. It was beautiful. Pictures were taken, bows were made, and all would talk about the King of the West from that day forth.

We had a great congregation.

We *had* a great congregation, I thought again. How was I now to lead them? I suddenly realized that I would not re-enter Hope Baptist for, at best, a very long time.

The ambulance pulled up at the hospital. The rear doors flew open. Two nurses aided in pulling me from the van. The same two nurses surrounded by a herd of friends and well wishers, whisked me into the hospital.

Wait!

The nurses were my secretary, Judy Carothers, and my friend Beth White from the King of the West charade. So much for feeling sorry for yourself, Ralph Showers. You have very good friends.

We played at this for quite a long while until I finally convinced them that I really ought to be turned over to the real thing. This party could have gone on forever. The thrill, the excitement of being among people who loved me had served to ease my pain more than all the earlier injected drugs. But the pain was coming back, so the party ended.

My God was a God of love, and my friends were His witnesses.

Orderlies and nurses, befuddled by our antics, took charge and wheeled me through the admittance procedure. Who are you? What are you? Why are you? How are you? Can you pay? All very efficient, taxing and tedious. An army of babies could be born right there at the admissions desk between choruses of who, what, how, and can you pay. I knew about hospitals, but I didn't like being there.

And then, turn about, wheel down a corridor, around a corner, and into the door marked "Burn Unit."

I had entered another world.

Pleasant, unrushed, cordial—everyone seemed to care. I was moved to a four-bed ward. Cleanly comfortable, it was not unlike the modern VA hospitals I had visited in my pastorate. The obvious care of the staff was everywhere. I knew that I was in for a hard and extremely painful experience. But, I thought, here they would treat me with dignity and concern. I was relieved.

As I entered the ward I could see that I would not be alone. One man lay sleeping in the far left bed. The front right bed was empty, but the bedstand and rack were filled with the artificial flowers and cards of a long stay. The two other beds were neatly ready for new occupancy.

Strangely, I was wheeled to the bed with the flowers. All of these tokens of love were for me. I started to cry. Word travels fast when you're having a bad time.

I was being taken care of, but what about Marilyn and the kids? I was being comforted and showered with love, but who was caring for my wife and family? I had support, but Marilyn had the burdens. Michael, Scotty, Mark, the ranch, the dream, the insurance, keeping house and home together—all these things that we had shared were now squatting on Marilyn's shoulders.

She had visited me in hospitals before, but never for anything so potentially serious. The doctors gave her some preparation for what she was to see, but nothing quite prepared her for the view of the red and black claw revealed when my protective sheet fell away.

She was shocked but not horrified. She handled it, and her handling of it made me able to stand all of the rest that was to come.

Marilyn went home knowing that this was to be a long-term siege. Her work was clearly laid out for her. Insurance papers had to be found and filled out. Arrangements had to be made for her to be able to be with me in Phoenix. So much to do, but she could do it, and she would do it.

And the ranch. She didn't know where I would be in terms of the ranch. Marilyn was not going to let the dream die until I made up my mind. She would keep the dream alive for me.

It was all I could do to keep me alive for me. What was going to happen to me?

"How many operations will it take me?"

It wasn't my voice. It was the rasped whisper of a young man being moved to the bed beside me. He was bandaged from head to foot. This young man, Steve, was to become my friend. I would never even learn his last name, but we would share a horrible month together.

He was just seventeen. Less than seven miles from the scene of my accident, on the same day, he was blown up with an exploding camp lantern and burned so badly he could hardly move. His pain, like mine, was nothing to what we were both to experience in the coming days.

We would talk for hours, lying there in our beds. Well, I would talk and he would listen and make sounds as best he could through vocal cords burnt to near uselessness. These low aching rumbles, aided by information from his visitors, was all I was to learn of him, but still we shared what seemed to be a lifetime.

Most of my thoughts were filled with the agony of my hands. Three of my fingers had to go almost immediately upon my entry to Maricopa County. Both thumbs and an index finger. The doctors were trying their best to save the rest.

Blood was not circulating properly through my arms. There was some concern about the fingers becoming gangrenous from lack of nourishment. Anticoagulants and other fluids were pumped hourly through me. I wanted the doctors to cut my hands off. Keeping those wretched talons was not worth another minute of pain. I could learn to make do without them, but I could not stand the incessant stabbing throb.

One day, perhaps the third, a finger moved. I didn't feel it, but a nurse was sure she had seen it. There was hope. I didn't want hope; I wanted them to cut the things off.

"You want 'em to amputate?" Young Steve winced as

much from the thought of the word as the strain of trying to say it.

"They hurt! Oh, how they hurt. Look, I haven't even got thumbs. What can I do with these things?"

"Things" was spit out like the corruption to which it referred.

"I'll probably lose another couple of fingers yet. And they hurt."

"What'll ya do without 'em?"

I hadn't really thought about that. What would I do without them? Probably get hooks, or—what was the word?—prosthetics or something.

The doctors had told me how bad the burns were. My back was a mess, but the shock had not impaired the spinal column. I would be able to learn to walk again. I would probably be able to stand up straight after a time. The hands were very bad. What should be done with those hands?

On my fourth day at Maricopa Hospital, Marilyn and my oldest brother, Jim, came to the ward with the doctor. Jim had seen my hands the night before. Marilyn was well aware of the state of my hands.

The doctor sat on the edge of my bed. He flipped through my chart as though it made some difference. After timeless seconds he spoke.

The doctors had decided what they felt should be done. Jim and Marilyn had been informed and agreed. How would Ralph feel?

"Cut them off," I said under forced breath.

"The fingers?"

"No, the whole mess!"

"That's your decision?"

"That's my decision. Cut them off!"

"Tomorrow, then." The doctor stood and left me with Marilyn and Jim. No one cried, it was the right decision, the one that needed to be made.

From the bed beside me I heard Steve's throaty sob. A

muffled moan, quickly concealed so as not to interrupt our moment of togetherness. We were all saddened, but the speechless boy was the only one to give his sorrow a voice.

But grief left me quickly. I will never understand what happened in my head, but all of a sudden it was an adventure. How do those prosthetic things work? When do I get them? What will they look like? They will certainly be better than three, maybe four, fingers. Will they be hooks?

Maybe I'm crazy. I've been told I was, by friends and strangers alike. But to me, it was like the proverbial spilled milk—where do we go from here? If I lost one leg, I could get a wooden one. Jim Dorsey had. If I lost my eyes, I could learn Braille or something. I guess it would be hardest for me to lose my hearing. But if I couldn't hear—well I'd learn to do something else. I'm a singer and I love to hear the wind and cars and birds. The point is, adversity breeds adventure and I was about to embark on an adventure.

It's hard to maintain exuberance in a hospital burn ward. Too many sad things always seemed to be happening. How the ward staff could handle such a constant barrage of sorrow and anguish was more than miraculous. They genuinely cared for their patients. They knew them all. Against everything, they seemed bright and thoughtful.

The man in the back left bed, the only occupant of the ward when I arrived, began to moan and thrash. Instantly the room moved with nurses and aides. Gently, but with professional speed, they placed him on a gurney and whisked him from the room. Steve and I were never to see him again.

We hadn't known him, had never spoken with him, had hardly thought of him. I knew he was critical—we were all critical—but nothing more. When he left, the room seemed oddly vacant. I missed him; I felt I had let him down.

I hadn't, of course. I couldn't really even see him over there, and he never made a sound except for his moans and hacking, gurgle-like cough.

Once I had tried to speak to him, but he didn't respond.

Or maybe I didn't hear him. I don't know if he lived or died. I prayed that I would see Steve walk or at least roll safely out of this ward of burned flesh. I don't think I could have borne to see him die.

Some hours later as I was being prepped for my journey to the scalpel the next morning, a new arrival was wheeled in, accompanied by a uniformed policeman. Later I was to learn he was a prisoner at the state correctional facility. Another inmate had thrown a Molotov cocktail into his cell, and he had caught the full force of the blast. My chemically induced sleep came on me too fast to be able to really see him across the ward from my feet.

My mind was a haze: the operation . . . all those people bothering over me . . . all this trouble I was causing.

From the very beginning I had had the feeling that I was inconveniencing everybody. Marilyn had taken several days off from school to be with me. C. A. McDonald had offered half a day's work and had had to cart the barn home without me. Now the Goehners and Marilyn were burdened with all my ranch responsibilities. What a mess I'd caused, not to mention all those houses without telephone service.

The worst thing was, nobody seemed upset with me. Everyone was considerate and loving. No one babied me, but no one blamed me either. It was a very comfortable tragedy. Only I seemed to feel I was a burden.

I didn't have much time to dwell on that. I was almost asleep. Tomorrow they were going to lop off my hands. I wondered how far up.

9

Hospital wards are never entirely quiet. Even at night, the sounds of orderlies wheeling their carts outside the door, the night nurses talking softly at their station, the occasional sound of a buzzer from a restless patient in another room all provide a constant cricketlike background noise to any ward. A burn ward is even more noisy. Here are the extremely critical patients, those who are in constant pain that even sleep cannot solve. A burn ward is never quiet, because no one is ever quite asleep.

I lay in the ward, hearing the sounds around me, dazed more from medication than want of sleep. My mind wandered, dreamed, remembered, doing anything but resting or thinking about my arms. They were to be removed this morning.

Mostly I dreamed of Rainbow Acres. I thought that Marilyn feared I would lose interest and let it die. I was not going to let it die. My mind moved me back a few weeks to a meeting with Grant Yeatman and his wife. We were at Ferguson's Restaurant, in Phoenix, discussing his taking over the pastorate at Hope Baptist, at least I was discussing the pastorate.

Mrs. Yeatman had an anxious, almost trembling edge to her voice. "Tell us what you're doing up at Camp Verde."

"Oh, well, really exciting things. But first let me tell you about Hope Baptist. The people there are just wonderful. The facilities are—"

"Some kind of a home for boys, isn't it?" Grant Yeatman looked every bit the solemn clergyman.

"What? Yeah, for handicapped boys. Now the actual sanctuary is large enough for—"

This went on for better than half an hour. I was programmed to sell them on Hope Baptist and they were set on hearing about the ranch. Usually I was more sensitive to this kind of cross-purpose conversation, but they were so perfect for the church and I was so excited about getting them there that I wasn't hearing.

Finally Jean Yeatman began to cry. The anxiety in her voice had been real. She was deeply troubled.

"Ralph, listen to me! Be quiet."

"What?" I was speechless. This was good because it finally gave her a chance to break in edgewise. I felt like an idiot.

Grant's otherwise cheerful voice had only seemed solemn under its heavy burden.

"You remember Ronnie?"

Ronnie Yeatman was their son. Now in his late teens, he was really an adult. Ronnie was retarded. He was a lovely boy and fairly easy to deal with as a child, but there was nothing they could do for him as a man. He would spend money he didn't have on phone-in TV ads, not realizing why it was wrong. He never had enough to do, and his parents were at a loss for new ideas. Once he bid on a piece of art at an auction, not realizing it would have to be paid for. Ronnie was physically a man, but mentally he was still a child. The Yeatmans were loving parents, but they were at a loss.

"We've looked everywhere for a good place for Ronnie. He's too old for any of the retarded programs." Jean's words were confused and upset. "You must help us. We trust you."

"Our ranch is for the handicapped," I said, instantly realizing the ridiculousness of my own words. "Of course Ronnie can stay with us. It will be a while before we're ready, but our ranch just now became a home for retarded adult men."

And so it had. Marilyn and I drove back north that same night to tell Larry and Joy. All this time we had been casting our fleece before the Lord, and now He was casting some back. We would build our ranch for mentally retarded young men. We would build it soon enough to be of aid to the Yeatmans and their son. I wasn't sure how we would do it, but the Lord would provide a way.

I was not sure what time it was, as I lay in my bed awaiting the nurses to come in to prepare me for the amputations. I knew the morning was approaching by the increase in noise outside the room. Soon they would give me the needle that would knock me out. Now I just lay and waited, half asleep, half daydreaming about the ranch.

We had told the Goehners. They had no objections. Only love and a "Let's do it!"

"How do we raise the money?" Larry was always so sensible.

"We ask our friends. We incorporate the place and then we ask our friends to send contributions."

As I have said, Rainbow Ranch was gone as a name, so Rainbow Acres was born.

"It sounds like a cemetery," Joy said, "or a housing tract."

We had settled on Rainbow because of the first incredible view. Acres was all that was available, so Rainbow Acres was it. Besides, it sounded like a pretty classy housing tract. Why not?

The next day we sat down and made up a list of three hundred friends and acquaintances. We drew up a letter announcing our venture and took it to a printer. Then we mailed it.

Then we started, not fighting, but playing footsies with the state and county licensing boards.

"We want a license."

"We can't give you one."

"Why not?"

"Because there aren't any for this kind of thing."

"Why not?"

"Because we don't have licensing for adult communities in Arizona."

"Why not?"

This could have gone on until Ronnie Yeatman was forty-five. Finally the state and county, unable to get together on a good reason not to let us have a license, just tossed up their hands and told us to go on and do whatever it was we were going to do. It is impossible to fathom the depths of a bureaucracy's inability to function until one has asked it to do something for the first time. This was not even my initial battle with what would become my greatest adversary—government.

Undaunted, we went forth. On September 3, 1973, we mailed our plea to friends. On October 25 I was lying in a Phoenix burn ward wondering if the ranch could be kept together. The Lord was to provide us a way, but what that way would be seemed mighty vague at the moment.

Also on October 25 the first of a stream of responses started to roll in—responses in the form of checks for more than enough money to pay off the legal fees required to get us going.

Also on October 25 a newspaper article mentioned my accident. More money came in—enough to compensate for the shortcomings of our insurance policies.

Saint Thomas had doubted three times. How many times would it take me?

"Reverend Showers? Are you awake?"

"Wha . . . ? Oh, yeah. What time is it?"

"It's pretty early. Come on. You gotta wake up so we can put you to sleep."

Suddenly it was clear. The great adventure was about to begin. Goodby, Ralph Showers the able-bodied. Welcome, Captain Hook.

It was the day nurse, a pretty young thing who made it all seem fine. She woke me gently and guarded me as the two strong boys moved me to the gurney. College students, I thought. They probably played for Arizona State.

I didn't seem to be hurting, though I knew I should.

"Please tell Steve I'm okay," I whispered, thinking how I would feel to wake up and find him gone. "Remember to tell Steve."

"Good luck." Husky words forced from nowhere, filled with love.

"Lie back down, Steve. He's going to be fine. We'll be back for you in a little while. Try to sleep some more." She had reassuring strength in her voice.

"See ya." Coarse, breathy sandpaper.

The two young men rolled me out. The hospital lowboy was carrying me to my adventure. Carrying me to a clean yellow room where I would be put to sleep. A sleep from which my hands would never awake.

"How high up?"

She knew what I meant.

"Just below the elbows. You remember; the doctor told you."

I guess he had. Why hadn't I remembered? Why did it matter?

I love you, Marilyn, I thought, as I fell under.

10

Two doctors worked on me—one for the right arm, one for the left. They would deal with my back later, on another day. Before they could do that, they had to do something called debriding. I wasn't sure what that was. Today they would just take the hands, cut off the pain.

Two skilled surgeons for one sore man. An arm apiece, both to be removed at the same place. The contest was obvious and unavoidable. I can only imagine the way it went.

"Lunch says I make a better cut."

"You're on!"

"Eat my dust, sucker."

Dinner rides on the sutures. I could imagine two skilled surgeons trying to find a way to be interested in this latest of hundreds or thousands of mangled passers-by. Professionals in a tedious, unending conveyor system of burned and broken people must surely have to search for some means to turn continuing horror away from its repetitive boredom. They could not allow themselves to become complacent, uninterested.

My right-hand man was to emerge the victor with steaks and beer for the perfect stitchery. My left-hand man had not let me down—just himself. His stitches were to get infected and would have to be redone.

I lay for hours in the wake-up room.

In the movies, the war-hardened sergeant wakes up after

the shelling to find himself in the post-op tent of a M.A.S.H unit. At first cheerful, he learns his legs are gone and breaks into tears while the future "Mrs. Sergeant" nurse runs to comfort her stricken warrior.

I felt none of that. I looked down the long white bed to see my bandaged stumps. Runted, but no longer withered. I was glad they were gone. Phantom pain? Yes, sometimes, but I knew it was a trick of my mind. I knew they didn't hurt anymore and the relief was profound.

It was over. Ralph was dead. Long live Ralph.

I didn't really even wrestle with the problem of no hands for about a day and a half.

Marilyn's parents had come into town a few days before the operation to give me support and to help their daughter through the ordeal.

They came in to see me in recovery and were struck by the idea that something was missing.

Later they told Marilyn they had this feeling I had lost something. It was ironic. They knew I had lost my forearms and hands. But the bandages were still there. Only shorter.

Well, of course there was something missing. They knew that. It just didn't register. They knew what had happened; they just didn't expect it to be quite like that.

I didn't expect it to be quite like that either. I had no regrets about the loss, just a sense of confusion about what to do with my arms gone.

Stumps.

"How do you feel?"

Stumps?

After an operation, a patient is expected to go into a depression. Before this surgery, I had been angry, I had been happy, I had been sad, but I had never been depressed. I scared the heck out of Marilyn. She was so used to me being up, optimistic to a fault. Now, here I was crashing to blubbering stupidity.

I couldn't help myself. I didn't want to be depressed. I wanted to take on the world, stumps flying.

Stumps.

I felt grief, like the loss of a loved one or dear friend. My upper arms had been widowed. My body had witnessed the passing of two of its members—a death without a funeral.

The head night nurse was a huge, efficient drill sergeant. Do this, do that, don't give me trouble. She was brisk and bossy: in to check the charts and change the I.V. bottles; out again with a stomping stride.

Nighttime was the tough time. We had no visitors to occupy our minds, no bustle in the outer hallways to distract us. We only had time to think, to feel the full force of anguish, to be lonely and alone.

I couldn't do it anymore. I was a wreck. I broke loose and sobbed until I couldn't see. Remorse, self-pity, grief, a sense of being cheated. I cried for all these things.

Enormous arms enfolded me. The efficient night nurse, the tyrant of the burn ward, pulled me up to her massive chest and held me. Clutching me to her for maybe twenty minutes, she let me bawl out my soul, a mother cradling her wounded son.

Such special moments are soon over. I would be all right. The next night the witch returned. How else do you cope on the graveyard shift in a graveyard?

Everything was now a problem to be solved. I was no longer able to grasp things, clutch, or touch things—no longer able to write or even blow my nose like other people.

The hospital bed tables were always stocked with boxes of tissue. How to use it? My stumps were sore, but flexible at the elbow. The wrappings gave them enough friction to hold soft objects pinched between. Since the accident other people had blown my nose for me; now I would do it myself.

Two or three tissues popped easily from the box. Rumpled up between my stumps, I lifted them to my nose. Three big blows and I was covered. Elated, I wiped my face and smiled for five minutes. Life was indeed worth living.

All was not perfect, but it was looking up.

I still didn't like having people feed me. I definitely didn't like the bathroom assistance.

If the nurse was cute and didn't seem to be too much in a rush, I could put up with the feedings. But that going to the toilet business took humility and turned it into humiliation.

A male nurse would get me into the bathroom and would then leave me to take care of business. Upon completion of this task I would reach out with my foot to ring a bell, summoning the man back into the room. This much I could take. Then I would rise up and he would wipe my bottom. This I could not stand. This was the greatest possible indignity. This would not continue.

It was time to visit the throne.

I summoned the male nurse. He had to hate this job, but was always polite.

He escorted me to the room and left me there, then stepped beyond the door to wait for my signal.

I sat there and took care of the necessities. I was not going to ring that bell. I reached over with my mouth to pull a big wad of paper from the holder onto my lap. Scrunching it up into a tight pile, I stood and closed the lid. This was it—success or total mortification.

Determined, I laid the mound of tissue on the throne and sat on it. Then I wiggled my bottom up, down, and sideways until I felt the job to be adequately done.

I picked up the paper, opened the lid, and flushed it down. Then I called the nurse. I was never to need his services again.

Today the toilet, tomorrow the shaver. Nothing could stop me now. All was an adventure and many more lay down the road, but for now I could blow my own nose, and wipe my own bottom. Give me another obstacle if you dare.

They did.

Three days after the amputation they took me to the debrider. Steve was to go, too. It would hurt, the doctors said, but the process was necessary in order to clean the burned skin and prepare healthy skin for grafting. The schedule called for two sessions a day for the next few weeks.

My back burns were to be the primary focus for a while. They were actually worse than my arms, having been in direct contact with the wire. The small of my back was an ashen ruin, like so much barbecued meat. The location of the burn was low enough to spare my spinal column, but situated so that I would have to learn to walk again.

I was to go to the debrider and then to physical therapy. Steve would follow the same route in reverse.

On that memorable first day, we were placed in wheelchairs and pushed down the corridor. After Steve had turned off into the physical therapy room, I was junketed into the next room for debriding.

"Please stop telling me how much this will hurt."

"We want you to be ready."

"What in heaven's name are you going to do?"

"Well, it's like a chemical bath. It, you know, kind of takes off the old layers of skin."

"Hoo, boy."

I entered the room. Not very big. It consisted of a large metal tank, like a small swimming pool. There were wooden steps that led to the lip of the tank and a seat on one end down below the side. At best it was five feet long by three feet wide and deep enough so that only my head and upper shoulders would rise above its confinement. Metal fixtures were set up to force in the bath.

It looked like a Jacuzzi.

The warm water and solution would probably sting my back and stumps. This wasn't going to be fun—twice a day for about three weeks.

I didn't think I would like this.

I could hear Steve in the therapy room as the bath began to fill.

"Oh! Oh, God! Oh, my God! Ahhch!"

I screamed, I cried, I begged for them to turn it off. Flashing pain—cruel, harsh, excruciating torture. I wanted to pass out. I wanted to die. I waited for relief.

My ears wanted to burst from my own shrieks.

I thought of the wire, my hands and back aflame with seventy-two hundred volts, scorching my muscles and exploding in my head. But this was worse, far worse, than the wire. That had been a piercing throb; this was wracking hell.

"God, help me! God, help me out of here!"

Tears etched canyons in my cheeks.

God had come to me on the barn. Where was He now?

God had said I would live, but for this?

Twice a day for about three weeks?

I could not think. I could not move. I could not get out of that boiling swirl of solution.

My flesh was raw. The meat on my bones was bare to the nerve.

And I screamed, a scream that drained my throat to a pitiful whine.

And then it was over.

Shivering, freezing, iceberg talons stung my frame. I trembled and whimpered through gasps for air. I was skinned venison hung to dry in a winter's wind. I was a frozen ember, an ash, a useless heap.

Nurses, faces drained from my torment, dried me off and lifted me to the chair. It was time for physical therapy.

Out in the hall I passed Steve on his way to that hell. He was a ghost. He shook with odious prospect. He had heard me. He knew what awaited him.

I could not look at his throbbing eyes.

We passed in the hall for the first of so many times to come. Dear God, comfort him.

I entered the physical therapy room. It looked like a polished wood playground. Parallel bars upon which to learn to stand, railed steps over which to drag, then pull, then move one's body, were scattered through the room like large-scale kiddy toys.

Steve's cries curdled through the paper-thin wall as I began my lessons. Hanging from the parallels, the agony of my friend's torment flashed its claws into my soul, and I withered.

Twice a day forever.

What could I do? I had to get out. I had to get better so I could get out.

The ranch, Marilyn, Mark, Scott, Michael, my friends—everything vanished from my brain. I pulled at the bars. The only escape was to walk, to get out.

Stumbling, the pain was nothing. It didn't matter. This was the pit, the bottom. From here it was up or death—suffocating, scorching death.

"Walk, darn it, walk! Stand up, stupid!" I chided myself.

Back in the room to await the evening session, we lay there, silently, hearing each other's breathing. All too soon we would be returning to the ordeal—me to scream, him to hear; him to scream, and me to hear. Neither was worse, for the memory was as harsh as the medicine.

God had said "Okay, Ralph," so I was to live. He had not promised me hands, and I hadn't thought to ask. He had not promised me freedom from anguish, but I had not thought anything could have been worse than the wire. He had only given me life.

A mortal, I had challenged God. I had told Him He had to let me live. Was I being punished for my brash arrogance? No! God was kind to me; He was letting me live to see what I could make of my dream.

Right: Ralph at his desk. **Below:** The grain barn Ralph was riding when he was burned: *(L to R)* Craig Lund and Peter Clark.

The entrance to Rainbow Acres, 1974 — the first days.

Ralph with his dog, Wiki.

Phillip Crowley in the woodshop.

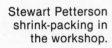

Stewart Petterson
shrink-packing in
the workshop.

Above: Ralph during Bible study with *(L to R)* Ronnie Yeatman, Betty Turner, Bob Hancock, Bill Poteete, David Butler, David Van Dyken, Ralph Showers, Mike Mattingly, Jeff Pitts.
Left: David Butler on the Garden Crew.
Below: First Board of Directors: *(L to R)* Ralph Showers, Thelma Warden, Rev. Grant Yeatman, Ed Bull, Larry Goehner, Charlotte Brown.

Ranchers during physical education class: *(L to R)* Jeff Pitts, Chris Grooms, Phillip Crowley, Bill Poteete, Gary Warner, Ed Simpson.

Three of the first residents of Rainbow Acres: *(L to R)* Rancher L. C. Coleman, house-parent Pat Needham, Rancher David Butler.

Marilyn and Ralph
on their wedding
day, 1960.

The Goehners
at New Hope Farm,
Washington: Joy, Larry,
Erik, and Allen — 1982.

Above: The Showers Family: *(L to R)* Michael, Marilyn, Mark, Ralph, and Scott at their home in Camp Verde, Arizona. **Below:** Coaching the Mustangs in Camp Verde. Far upper left: Scott and Mark Showers. Far right: Ralph Showers. Michael Showers is in the second row, second from the left.

11

The days staggered on, with their unyielding waits between sessions with the dreaded debrider. It never got better. One never gets used to pain of that sort. It is not like the throb of a tooth that can be dismissed by dreaming of better times.

Steve and I existed between baths, unable to think beyond the tub, the chemical vat.

We never talked about it. We didn't have to. We rarely talked at all to each other during that time. We were the same person; there was nothing to say.

Visitors came and went, bringing momentary cheer. Marilyn, of course, came often. Her life had settled into a routine of school, the chores, then down to Phoenix. On Fridays at 2:30, the boys would get out of school and come home to packed bags for the trip to their grandmother's house, so Marilyn could spend the weekend around the hospital.

She was as much a fixture as I. This high-spirited woman who grew dizzy in hospitals was busying herself helping the nurses, changing bandages, and applying ointment to the parade of strangers.

Wives and mothers of the other patients were falling beneath the burdens of their loved ones. Marilyn gave them strength. Marilyn's strength gave me strength.

But still the baths went on.

Cards and letters, all bright and cheery, passed over my

bed. Some were funny; some, loving; some were reminders of past friendships that awaited renewal. All forms of good wishes came before my eyes to be read and held.

"God has cursed you. You are a sinner and a wretched creature!"

Unsigned and scrawled in a hate-filled hand, this letter saddened me. Who would write such things? What poor sick soul could hold so much hate?

Marilyn, brothers Jim and Bob, and Mother would try to screen out the handful of vicious mail before it reached me. They had accidentally seen one such note and hurried to keep others from me. One had passed through their caring net.

Strangely, it had not upset me. I knew that God loved me, and I felt sorrow for the author. What loneliness he must feel to reach out in such a way. I prayed for this person.

Eddie Prettyman came by often and stayed to share my wife's load. He and Bill Beamon would provide the shoulders that Marilyn would need when she left my bedside.

An old friend and fellow preacher, Walter Thompson, would bring me walnuts with notes inside some of the shells—little messages that would surprise me every time with hope and joy.

I feared returning to the tank, but my spirits never fell so low as that night when I had cried in the arms of the terrible nurse. The future was becoming clear. The doctors still had to do the grafting on my back. That was to come as the baths were done.

I was to be given a special bed. They called it a "striker" but I had no idea why. It sounded like fun. It could rotate on some kind of ball bearings so that I could be spun over. How bad could that be? My own personal roller coaster!

The hospital chaplain, Reverend Fred Crumb, visited me often. Though of a different church, he gave me comfort. He had been the man who helped explain my situation to Marilyn those long three weeks before. A long-term friendship blossomed between us.

Many other friends from Hope Baptist, from all over Arizona and California, dropped by to share a minute with me. Larry and Joy came too, of course, and that gladdened me. The boys would send me notes, wishing they could visit, but understanding that they could not.

Long hours in the physical therapy room had taught me how to use my back and legs again. Constant practice with weights on my stumps and arms gave me strength. The sensitive care of the staff got me through the baths.

Then they brought in the striker.

"What is that?"

"That, Ralph, is your new bed."

"That, nurse, is weird."

"No, it's a striker bed."

"What are the straps for?"

"So you don't fall out."

She must have been a practical nurse, because she had a practical answer for everything.

"What am I going to do? Thrash about?"

Was this a new enemy?

"No, but we're going to turn you bottom side up and we don't want to break you."

That seemed fair.

"Why do you want to turn me over?"

"So the doctor can work on your back."

She was informative, but only if you pried. I thought she could have stood up well under the third degree. Perry Mason would never have gotten a confession out of this one.

"Does it hurt?"

"No!"

That answer I liked. I had had enough hurting for ten people.

The contraption was a big round thing, like a great wheel with a bed in it. The bed part looked all right. It was the wheel that confused me.

"In you go."

I didn't really have a choice, but this thing intrigued me. Besides, I was ready for an adventure, and the nurse said this thing didn't hurt. How bad could it be?

In I went.

They strapped me down. Not just my middle, but my chest and feet as well. Then they turned me over.

"Hello, floor."

The nurse bent down to look at me, hanging there two feet from the tile.

"How's the weather down there?"

"Not bad. When do you turn me bottom side down? This side is done."

"In a few days."

I didn't believe it.

I had had pain. It was impossible for them to top the pain of the baths. But I had never had boredom. Not just what-to-do-now, but totally helpless, powerless boredom. Before, I could turn my head, see things, take in all the activity of the ward. I could look over at Steve, look out the door, feel a part of the world. Now I hung. The floor was clean. No ants or bugs marched by, no clouds formed interesting patterns to find pictures in, no dots waited for me to connect them. Nothing.

There was a mirror that could permit me to see a visitor when one came, if that person stood just right and didn't move around too much. Other than that I could see only the blank ceiling and myself.

How long can a person stand to look at himself? I have never been narcissistic. I'm not bad looking, but I'm not all that interesting either. How can Marilyn stand to look at that face so long? How can she love me? How can she stand to be near this crippled wreck? What if she can't?

My heart clenched. I couldn't endure this, not any more. I had withstood an eternity of baths, but now I was panicking for nothing. I was staring into my own eyes, the ceiling-floor pulsating, coming nearer. I saw the sweat form over my eyebrows to spread over my face.

She wouldn't want me to touch her. She would baby me. She would leave me.

I was on the wire again. My brain shot from place to time to memory. My veins convulsed inside of me. I was scrambling for some tiny proof that Marilyn would not leave me. My own sweat rained down upon the face staring up at me.

I remembered that long-ago Christmas and the progressive dinner. That winter had been Casanova's delight.

Those first dates, while I was also dating two others, she had to have loved me from the start, I reminded myself. How else could she have allowed herself to continue dating this three-timer? But then the man she had loved had had two arms, and hands to hold her cold feet. Now he was strapped and hanging from a bed staring at himself, a cripple.

Marilyn was brave when she came to the hospital. She seemed loving and caring, but what was she thinking? How could she imagine herself making love with a man with no arms? How could a man with no arms make love?

Never in my life had I allowed myself maudlin self-pity for more than a moment. Now I wallowed in it.

The doctors wouldn't turn me over because of the pressure it would put on my back. They had no idea of the strain I had on my heart.

12

And then it was over.

The rearranging of raw skin, cleansed by the horrible baths.

The scraping, the stitching, the pulling and kneading, the trembling and fear, the claustrophobic staring at a pulsating floor, the terrible, echoing stare of my own eyes— it was all over. Nobody knew what I had gone through. Nobody realized that the chipper smiling face that now turned up toward the ceiling—that distant, solid ceiling— had just been through such an ordeal.

To be held down by gravity rather than restrained from it was a sensation beyond words. My heart, which had hung down in my chest, now settled back comfortably in its crevice. My head and neck, enervated from having held my whole body rigid and in place for so long, sighed into the pillow. My back was sore with a glorious ache that comes as relief from torturous pain. My eyes focused up, not on reflections, but on friends. Exhausted, worn to a frazzle, but alive and thriving, thank you very much. The world was well again.

There would be problems. Certainly life was no kind master that would protect me, body and soul, for the rest of my days. Hardships were to follow. Stress, even pain lay in wait for me, but the worst had finally passed. All else would be adventure. All else, at its worst, would be bearable. Now, get me those hooks, and let's get on with it.

Marilyn, Eddie Prettyman, Bill Beamon, my family, the chaplain—all of my friends gathered around me. It was a time of rejoicing, a time for them to celebrate Thanksgiving, less than a week away. To celebrate my one-day furlough I was to spend Thanksgiving at the Prettymans'. For me it was a time to exalt the wonders of a world gone awry now back on its orbit.

"When do I get my hands?"

It didn't matter who I was talking to. Anybody might have a scrap of information, a hint, a clue. No nurse was safe from my questions; no nurse was immune to my enthusiasm.

"Let me at those things! When do I get those things? Say, doctor, can you lend me a hand?"

"The prosthetics man comes tomorrow."

"Why not today?"

"He comes once a week."

"Will I get my hands tomorrow?"

"Of course not. You have to be fitted for them. Then they have to be made." The nurses enjoyed my anticipation and shared in my exuberance.

"How long'll it take to make them?"

"Well, now, the doctor has to be sure you're ready first."

"I'm ready. You're looking at a ready person. How do you hold a hammer in a hook?"

"You don't."

"Wrong! I'll find a way."

"I'll bet you will."

"You're darned tootin'."

"Now listen, Ralph." It was the day nurse. "The doctor won't let you have arms until the swelling goes down. If you try to use prosthetics too soon you can reopen the wound. It may be six or seven more months. This doctor doesn't know you like we do."

"Well, come with me."

"What?"

"Tomorrow, when I see this guy, come and tell him that I'm okay."

Tomorrow came. I was just starting to realize that tomorrows do tend to come. I had lost sight of that fact for several weeks. Baths came, treatments came, eternal hours staring at my own face on the floor came, but tomorrow never seemed to come. Tomorrows were when things got better, and finally I was becoming aware that tomorrows lay before me in a vast vista. Today was the first tomorrow, so many lay ahead.

The night nurse, that harbinger of efficiency, wore a protective aura of untouchable control and detachment. That wondrous enigma who had held me through my tears and then returned to cold expertise, wrapped my stumps a little tighter, a little more carefully, with a hidden prayer for my tomorrow.

The problem with tomorrow is that even after it arrives there can be so much of it to wade through before the big moment gets here. At six-thirty when I woke up, it was tomorrow, but the prosthetics man didn't show until after noon. Tomorrow takes forever.

"Don't get your hopes up, Ralph," my friendly ex-bottom-wiping male nurse cautioned.

"Now, it may not be today," warned an intern.

"Hey, man, if not today, then tomorrow."

Wrong. Today was tomorrow.

They were being kind. They knew the routine and the cautions the doctor had to follow. They knew the odds against my getting arms the first time through. They knew, but they also wanted me to get those arms.

I spent the day wheel-chairing through the burn unit, stopping to speak with other patients, trying to give them a sense of the light I had found at the end of this tunnel of pain. Marilyn had been so fantastic in sharing her strength with patients and their families, I wanted to help too, to ease the burdens, to clear up the uncertainties. Some had been severely burned, some less so; a few had lost an eye or a limb like me, but few had had it quite so rough. I wanted to serve as an example that it all could work out. I hope they got some relief, because sharing with them gave me comfort.

I went back to my room to wait.

"Ready to go, Reverend Showers?"

"Fantastic."

"Good luck, sir." My young friend's harsh whisper sent a thrill through me. His bandages were mostly off and he would leave soon. I would never see this brave boy again, but he will always fill my prayers.

"Thanks, Steve."

As the male nurse wheeled me to the hall, from doorways and passages the staff would offer hopeful smiles and warm words. Then the head day-nurse took up cadence beside me, while another joined us on my left. A young candy-striper, who had enjoyed talking with me, pushed open the wide doors from the burn ward and followed me out. Look out, world. Here come Ralph Showers *et al.* What we had here was a parade.

"Remember your number, Reverend Showers."

What number? Oh yeah, the one on my wrist. 28040094. With all those numbers, I wondered if they had started from one. There couldn't be that many patients. Why did I need to remember my number?

Into the physical therapy room we marched—an entourage. Others were there from other parts of the hospital. I alone came equipped with a cheering section. I thought about these kind people beside me. The burn ward staff sees the worst of it, but gives the most of themselves. God bless them.

The other amputees and I formed a line.

"Circle your wagons," someone quipped. "Here comes the Indian."

And in he came, brisk and straight, a Prussian officer dressed in smart whites, frown lines etched all over his face.

This man was tough, efficient, and very impersonal. He marched down the line, chart at the ready, pen cocked for action.

"17940034, hmm, not ready yet. Two weeks." A flash of pen on chart. One down.

"2529670, hmm, not ready yet. Next week." Another flurry of pen on chart. Two down.

He strode to a patient. He bent at full attention, lifting an abbreviated leg or arm like a musket in a parade line. This was no good; he might not give me my arms. He would go home and sip sherry, and I would be left to wiggle my bottom on a mound of mashed paper. I couldn't live with that.

"28040094."

Gulp.

My escort hurried in front of me, pulling the doctor out of his stride. Hurried muffled words followed by gruff retorts.

"No, we can't do that. These stumps won't reduce." He pulled at my upper arms to make his point.

"Two weeks at best."

"I'll make you a deal."

"Pardon me?"

"I'll make you a deal." I wasn't leaving with just a flurry of pen and a "hmm" like the others. Besides, I was getting good at making deals on a higher level than this.

"You let me get my arms right now; do the molds and all that kind of stuff."

"Hmmm." He was not buying this.

"Now wait; this is for science. Research, you know."

"Hmmm." Science and research hit the right spot.

"If you do that, I promise not to go to any rehabilitation program or anything. For science's sake," (it had worked before) "I'll be a guinea pig. We can find out how well a man can get along trying to adjust to new arms by himself."

"Not go to rehab? Hmmm."

"What a wonderful experiment." The nurses were right in there pitching.

"You are very sure you want to do this?" We had him.

"Yeah, I want to do this."

"Yeah, let him do it." Long live the nurses.

"Well, all right, then."

"Really an excellent experiment," chimed in the support team.

How many patients have the benefit of a Greek chorus when going before the doctor?

"Well, should we give him a wrist?"

"Oh yeah, gotta have a wrist, definitely need a wrist. In fact, two wrists, yeah, one for each arm."

"No, no, I can't give you two wrists. You don't really—"

"Oh, yes. I must have two wrists. That's the deal. Two arms with one wrist each and no rehab."

"Yes, he certainly should have two wrists."

We definitely had him. The perfect clincher for an academician's heart—a research paper. It was like an addiction; a scientist cannot resist the chance at a research paper.

"All right, that will be fine." His Prussian aloofness was wavering slightly. He composed himself. "31497862, hmm."

I was to have arms. I was to have wrists. I was joyous. How do you work these things? Where is the movie? I want to see a movie. Do you have a book? How about a pamphlet? Can I see one? What do wrists do? Oh man, I can't wait!

Tomorrow was today and today was terrific. Tomorrow I would start in on the molding and fitting. Come on, tomorrow!

Life, so desolate, so bleak just two days before, was now loving and brilliant. The day after tomorrow was going to be another tomorrow filled up with Thanksgiving. Boy, was I thankful. I was going to get arms, and I was going on furlough.

Thanksgiving Eve was a full day of casts and measuring. These things were going to strap to my back. My back muscles and shoulders would make them work. I went to bed, totally bushed, totally happy.

I was to check out at nine in the morning. By six I was up, shaved, dressed, and sitting on the bed. I hadn't seen the boys for five weeks. I still had no arms, but I was going to wrap my stumps around each one of them and squeeze. I missed them.

They had never seen me without hands. What would they think? Our children had been born—first Mark, then Scott, then Michael—into an environment where sharing and communicating had been the norm. We were not a family of overreactors. But they were still children. This might frighten them.

Marilyn had kept them constantly aware of my progress. They were assured that Dad would be all right; he would be well and healthy. They had been told about the amputation and about the hooks. Marilyn had done everything possible to include them, to keep them posted, but still, how one hears about things and how one actually experiences them are two separate realities.

Nine o'clock came.

I left the room and walked to the nurses' station. The chaplain was there speaking with a nurses' aide. We greeted each other and the aide started to fill out my furlough papers for me.

"Don't do that!"

The chaplain's voice was perhaps a little too sharp, but the aide understood. The chaplain reached behind the desk and took a rubber band from the drawer. Wrapping it around twice, he fastened the pen to my right stump.

I signed myself out.

Trepidation moved in upon my joy. I was rounding the corridor that led to the waiting room. The boys would be waiting. Marilyn would move back and let them greet me.

"Daddy!"

I swallowed hard.

All three pounced upon me: hugging me, kissing me, loving me.

"Boy, are your arms short." "Wanna wrestle?" "Hey, we got him now; he can't grab us."

They had their daddy. They couldn't give a hoot about his arms. All they wanted was me.

Thanksgiving at the Prettymans' will live long in my memory. The food was wonderful, and the room was replete with joy. Happy talk and gentle roughhousing with the boys. By eleven-thirty I was beat. Home for me was the hospital and, boy, did I want to go home.

I staggered in around one-thirty and passed out, only barely glimpsing the smug smile from the passing night nurse. I was happy, but I was dead tired.

No matter what, I had to get out before Christmas.

13

I had tasted freedom and it had been sweet. That Thanksgiving escape from the confines of the hospital was the break-off point. I had to get out of that hospital, get back to work, get back to the ranch.

The Rainbow Acres letter to our collective friends was paying off. Responses were wonderful, all bearing money and warm prayers for our enterprise. There was money to pay for the ranch's legal fees and for minor land improvements. Money to pay for a new letter, a larger mailing, swept through our mailbox and straight through the checkbook. But was it in vain? Was it too late?

Larry and Joy had spent hours with Marilyn what-if-ing. What if Ralph has lost interest? What if he can't keep up his end? What if it's over? Without Ralph, what's the point?

They didn't want it to be over. They wanted it more now than before. But, what if Ralph didn't?

Nobody talked to me about these doubts. All visits were cheerful and brimming with news; everything was going fine at home. This money came in; that letter arrived; this friend sent his best. Never did anyone ask if I still had my dream.

I did.

I had my dream and the memory of a vision. Standing with my back arched against the fires of torment, I had found a momentary peace, a solitude, an awareness. God had spoken to me in a language I could clearly understand:

"Okay." Okay, I would live. Okay, I would see my children grow. Okay, I would be with Marilyn. Okay, I would see the ranch.

I had paid for my end of the bargain, but I had had the long end of it. How many mortals have a guarantee of life for any price? There is no guarantee for how long. Certain conditions filled, I could die at any time. But, those conditions filled, I would die a happy man.

From my hospital bed, I had shared this knowledge with my wife. She had been startled a bit, and amazed at what I was saying, but she understood. She knew it was true. She could believe in my unbelievable miracle. She was awed by it, but not by me. Marilyn knew that, through my experience, I would be able to get through my ordeal at the hospital. But what about afterwards? I was a man, her husband, and she feared for, or at least was concerned about, who I would be upon leaving treatment.

During these long weeks Marilyn had an experience too, but nothing so dramatic as high-tension wires and windows to God. Something more basic, simpler, and perhaps more deeply personal. She had been carrying out her routine of work and hospital visitations. Things were hectic but predictable. I was always in the middle of some form of pandemonium: amputation, baths, striker. Something began to wear on her. She wasn't sure how long she could maintain the pace.

As time had gone on, and the burden became mightier, she had found releases. Eddie Prettyman had lent her his caring shoulder to lean against or sob into. Her good friend from years before, Robbie, had called to offer aid and had held onto the phone through Marilyn's most heartfelt unburdening—a wonderful, solid cry into a telephone to a friend who would understand. These things and more had offered her solace on a day-to-day basis throughout the early struggle.

At last it was too much. After so long and so much, a shoulder or a friend was no longer enough. The decisions were too many, the anguish too great, the strength too often spent.

It was the morning the decision was to be made whether or not to amputate my arms. She drove her car from my mother's house in Phoenix to visit me. Much later, Marilyn would sit by my bed and share with me her story of that long drive. The long, short drive.

The doctor had asked her to be at the hospital by 7:00 A.M. She got into the car to make the now-familiar journey. What would the decision be? She should have been filled with anxiety at the thought of what might lie ahead.

Never has Marilyn not believed in the teachings of the Bible. Her earliest memories were of her father's services, Bible school, the give-and-take of church life and church work. It was all around her, all through her, and she loved it. But she was never one to think of God or speak of God in a familiar way. She knew and believed God's words, but was not a Scripture quoter.

That morning the promises of the Bible floated through her mind. Those simple teachings of God's love for mankind entered her heart and rode with her to my side.

"God loves you."

"He cares for you."

"Lo, I am always with you."

The basics. The pure songs that settle deep within a person and help make one Christian. From the first promise, the day regained hope and Marilyn regained strength.

She told me, "I began to realize how clear it was that day. You know how it is after a rain, when everything stands out at you."

For the first time since she had begun her drive to the hospital, she became conscious of her surroundings. A man was mowing his yard along the side of the road. A kid was riding his bike. Flowers were blooming all along the way. But the neatest thing of all was the reality of the promises softly moving up from some distant recital in her past.

That moment, that morning's drive, will carry Marilyn

through her life. It will always be with her to give her peace as it did on that most peaceless day.

Neither of our appreciations of God, our faith or belief, had changed. We still had a deep commitment to Him. But, now He was unquestionably real to both of us. Our lives had been touched, dramatically, but not changed.

Marilyn and I had been happy . . . most of the time.

I recalled the problems our marriage had had a few years before when I became very involved in my work. I moved as I found newer challenges. Marilyn and the growing family followed. I immersed myself in my work, eventually to the exclusion of my family. Finally it reached a head in Ewa Beach, Hawaii.

So involved, so completely absorbed in the battle to save the bowling alley for the kids, I had lost track of Marilyn. She told me so in terms that made the problem clear to me. I had to work this out, but how? Everywhere at Ewa Beach there were jobs for me to do. The church was growing so fast, and things were happening so fast, that there was no place for us to go to be alone.

Marilyn and I are very strong people. There has never been a sense of her being less than I. When we have something to say, we bring it right on out. But there was no time to speak. Things around us assumed great importance. It was a daily confrontation of triviality. Petty things seemed to find time to upset us, while the serious problem hung back like a threat. We picked at each other. We were miserable.

Finally the storm hit. We either had to thrash this out or separate. I made a reservation at a hotel in Waikiki, and we set off to settle things or end our marriage.

We checked in and were given a beautiful room with a spectacular view. We were too upset to notice our surroundings.

For two days we talked, we cried, we wrote out lists of all those things that galled us about the other. We read the

lists, we talked, we cried. We wrote out more lists. We checked out. We were in love.

We had learned about each other. About feelings and
sore points, weaknesses and strengths that neither of us
were aware of in the other. We had swallowed a lot of pride
in those forty-eight hours, because we had so much to swal-
low. But we came out of that room, not just married, but a
couple. Each with our own personality, both with a strong
sense of our unity.

Many years have been spent since then consciously and
wholeheartedly working on items from the lists made in
that beautiful room. And a stronger marriage has grown
between two adults who knew and loved each other, despite
and because of life.

Now we were growing again, even closer because of our
new needs, our new experiences, our new commitment to
God and our dream ranch. Our children were our lives,
and our lives had been strengthened by their support and
love in this trying time. The ranch and our children were
our future—a future bright with our mutual care.

At Thanksgiving, after dinner and before the onset of
exhaustion, some important words had been spoken: "Marilyn, we have got to get me out of there. I've got to get back
to work. The Yeatman boy doesn't have a place to grow in."

No, Marilyn and Larry and Joy need not have worried
about Ralph. The dream was still alive and well and living in
Ralph Showers. Marilyn would tell Larry. Larry would tell
Joy. The dream was on. I had to get out.

Back at the hospital I spent one day recouping. The next
morning I awoke early. I had to shave.

It was the routine. Every morning at six-thirty the doctor
would make his rounds. He would check charts and scribble
notes of improvement or decline. The doctor was the way
out. He was the one who would say if I was ready.

I got up at five-thirty. I washed and shaved and put on a
clean pair of pajamas. I did whatever I had to so that I

would look bright and healthy to this man with the key to the hospital door.

Marilyn came to hear the verdict. While we waited, I hugged her with my stumped arms, strengthened by weights and exercises. I wanted to squeeze us together into one being. I failed, but loved the attempt.

The troups filed in—the ward doctors and nurses, my friends and therapists.

"Ralph, you can leave tomorrow."

"When do I get my arms?" Important things first. I was going to leave tomorrow anyway.

"You pick them up on Tuesday. Good luck."

Good luck . . . you dear people do not realize that you are my good luck. Your care and love helped to bring me through this. I am grateful not just for the help with physical problems, that was your job, but I am grateful for the care you showed for the mental and emotional carnage my soul has endured. You, with your Greek choruses and midnight hugs, your love of people and five-thirty wake-up calls—you have saved my life. You are kind, kind people whom I will always cherish in my heart, though I may never see you again. God bless you, you beautiful white-robed Samaritans.

I did not say these things. I just coughed back my tears and said, "Thank you."

Then I thought of Steve, since departed for home and a full rich life. He had shared so much with me. His rasping, guttural, pain-filled voice had given me so much hope. His daily, mutual suffering in the baths, unspoken of but real. I wondered where he was. He is my brother. I have been everywhere with him. I love him.

I looked to the refilled bed where he had spent those torturous days and could no longer hold my tears. I cried for the love of him, for these gathered helpers and loved ones, for those poor souls who have passed into the ward and into their deaths. I cried in joy at my new life before me, and in sorrow for the life I was leaving. Tomorrow I was leaving. Thank you, God, for yesterday.

14

My tears had been shed. The soaked pillow had been removed and the bed remade. I rose early, excited, my sorrow past. I couldn't wait to be going home. In a few days it would be Christmas.

In fewer days it would be Tuesday—Arms Tuesday, the day of the hooks. I could scratch again if I itched.

Today it was Sunday. I was going home.

The greeting was tumultuous. I walked in the door of the double-wide trailer and into the arms of Larry, Joy, the kids, and four-fifths of the known world at the same second. We rejoiced together and they left. I was home.

Mark, Scott, and Michael watched Marilyn feed me dinner, more with interest than pity. I was uncomfortable, but, this was the way it was to be, for the while. I was home and would eat with my family. We would all learn to get used to me.

After dinner there was light roughhousing with the boys, along with some TV, and then they went off to bed. Marilyn and I talked awhile. Not about anything; just talk. The evening grew later. Marilyn and I headed off for bed.

Now I would know. Fears from nights of hanging over my self-pitying reflection tried to force their way back into my brain. Now I would know. How changed was I? How much of a husband could I be?

So much that I had known required hands. So much. Now I would know. But not from fear. This was to be an adventure. I can always accept the challenge of an adventure.

Marilyn only told me that my stump arms were soft. Much softer than hands. Much more gentle. Now I knew.

Life was wonderful. Monday came and I walked the ranch, every inch of it. Planning, dreaming, enjoying the wildness of it and the beauty, Larry and I shared this day.

All of our aspirations for the future flooded out upon the ground whereon we walked. The industrial center should be over there. No, we ought to concentrate on agriculture. The first houses should be over there. Yes, that will take the best advantage of the road. The barn needs to be moved over to that hill so the corral can go over there. Right.

Casually we talked about the barn. The accident had happened so long before that I didn't even think about the barn as its cause. Marilyn had told me that some men from the Arizona Power Service had come to look at it. They had measured it and walked around it, filled pages of notes about its relative dimensions, then left.

Life was ahead; the barn was just a barn. The past was a vision in the cloudless sky.

I wondered when the boom would drop. When would I have to pay the piper for all the destruction I had wrought upon the Verde Valley? I had ridden a barn, burned up the wires, made the utility company change their pole and wires, and left a house without telephone and electricity. Oh, well. When the bill came, it would come. I would deal with that later. I hoped it wouldn't cost too much.

For now, Larry and I were busy trying to figure a way to get this ranch back on its feet.

"We can put in hay over there for the horses."

"Yeah, good."

"Then corn and a huge garden over there."

"No. The industrial center has to be there. That's how we're going to pay for this place."

"We can pay for it with produce. That would be a better job for the ranchers. Out of doors and all."

"Well, I think there's more variety in indoor work with the outdoor stuff as a treat."

"Ralph, look at those horses."

"Boy! We have to get some horses."

On and on into the night. The future was lying on a high desert field. Wild Indian horses chewed on the mesquite and tall grass above the hill where the barn would go. I was happy and growing tired—and a little impatient for Tuesday.

Tuesday came. All those tomorrows I had learned to count on coming always seemed to come. This tomorrow was Tuesday and Tuesday was here. Arms Tuesday. Arms today.

"What is a stump sock?" I was incredulous.

The clerk at the prosthetics place in Phoenix walked away on his two good legs and returned with a roll of gauzy-looking cloth in one of his two good hands.

"They keep your stump ends warm, and protect them from chafing in the prostheses."

He smiled a genuine smile through a set of very good teeth.

I decided he was probably a good man.

I stuck out my arms with a show-me-how look, and the clerk obliged by unrolling two long white heel-like socks. Well, what had I expected?

He pulled them on my arms.

"Do they come in any colors?"

"No. Just white. No one will see them anyhow."

"Oh?"

"Well with your arms on and a shirt."

"Long sleeve?"

"Naturally."

"Hmmm."

He left again for a minute, while I mulled over hot Arizona summers in long-sleeve shirts.

"Is that them?" I asked when he returned.

"Yes, sir. Made to order. Now go easy with these. The

doctor told me you're only a month or so past your operation."

"Gimme!"

Eagerly, I laid out the strapped plastic appendages. It took me twenty minutes (of course, I wouldn't let the clerk help) to get the back straps in place. Everything had to be just right if the metal claws were to open on command.

Once set, I slipped my arm ends into the thin tubelike forearms. I was ready. I lifted the beige plastic wings and pushed forward from my back.

I thought I was done with hurting. I was wrong. The soft, sensitive ends were a thin shield against still raw nerve ends. I screamed their protest.

"Are you all right?"

"I'm fine. Oh, yeah. No problem. Just kinda pinched myself. Wrap those up. I'll take 'em home. Right, no problem."

"You're sure?"

"Sure, I'm sure. Say, don't mention this to the doctor, will you? He may get the wrong idea, okay?"

He just nodded, wrapped my bundle, and showed me to the door.

I was going to learn to use those things if it killed me. Based on my initial attempt, it just might.

The hooks were not really hooks as such. They were more like pinchers. The idea was, I was to put torque on the forearm by pushing my stumps into the sockets, while pulling back on my shoulder muscles to draw a thin cable. This cable pulled against a spring mechanism that opened the crooked pincher. The amount of tension on the pinchers, created by the addition of thick rubber bands, determined my holding power.

I took off all but one rubber band. It still hurt.

I had known the instant I saw the arms in the shop that I could do it all. I was just going to whip those things on, and that would be that. I was learning humility faster than I was learning sense. I couldn't do anything. I couldn't pick up anything. I could hardly even get the darned things on.

But it was an adventure.

One whole week passed. Pushing and hurting, pushing and hurting. Taking them off, putting them on—over and over again. Picking up paper, pencils—anything the single, rubber-band muscle was strong enough to hold.

And then there were the wrists. The hooks were set into the forearm-like attachments in a socket wrench. The holder could turn along a track to any direction I wanted. All I had to do was release a spring and turn the hook. I had flexibility. I could scratch places I could never get at before, if I didn't mind a little pain in the process.

Two-hook, simultaneous operations were tricky. My back and shoulder muscles ached from their new uses. Opening the clasps at the same time, or at different times—all this required a strange series of contortions. It was no good if I looked too weird in the process, I thought. These things were to be hands. They were going to draw attention, but as little as possible.

As the throb subsided I would add another elastic muscle.

By the end of ten days I had it down. I could grab, turn, angle, lift—anything. I had them figured down to a "T"— all except for one black bump on each hook. I could not figure out that silly rubber blurp.

When I first got back from the hospital, Marilyn was still working at Head Start. Between my inability to do anything completely for myself and my needing to be shuttled around for doctors or ranch business, Marilyn was being run ragged. Finally we decided that the insurance and our savings were sufficient to handle our expenses, so Marilyn left the school. Except for her pragmatic worries about finances, she was overjoyed at the prospect.

In the interim between the decision and her actually being home full time, I would make lists for myself of the new things I would learn to do. I wanted Marilyn home because it would be best for everybody, but I didn't want her to have to cater to me.

First I had to learn to use the telephone. Now, the hooks

made dialing easy, but lifting and cradling the receiver was a problem. The addition of one of those secretarial shoulder/chin supports helped. It was the double-wrist action that made the day. I would open one hook, preset to the right angle, at first painfully wide, to remove the receiver. Then I would transfer it to my other hook, preset at the wrist for placing it properly to my ear.

Opening doors with knobs created for palm and finger control was tough. The metal clamps could not get any traction on the metal knobs and would just slip. Electrician's tape around the knob provided a tractable surface so that no fire would find me a trapped victim.

All this time I was periodically visiting my doubting Prussianesque prosthetics doctor at the hospital. I was amazing him with my progress, but I never asked about the rubber bumps. I was going to figure that out for myself.

I was visiting other doctors as well, but for my back, never for my arms.

All this driving made me want to relearn that essential skill for Arizona's immenseness. Marilyn was still stuck with regular chauffeur duties that took away from other essential chores.

Automatic transmission took care of shifting difficulties. My feet were fine, so the brakes and gas were no problem. The ignition key was simple. But I couldn't steer the thing. I could never get a grip on the wheel, and driving by the cross bar was unsafe in panic situations. Besides, I had to be able to drive all cars, no matter the width or configuration of the wheel. I was going to have to be inventive.

I needed some kind of knob that could be affixed to the wheel—any wheel—without a lot of screwdrivers and tools. Something that wouldn't harm a friend's or a rented car. What to do?

In idle conversation one day with a friend, John Downs, I mentioned my driving situation. The challenge appealed to him. In a matter of days he got back to me with a contraption a friend of his had invented. It was a metal rod fixed with spring-loaded hooks that was adjustable to any steering wheel width, with an eyelet on the end for me to pinch. It was fantastic. The world's highways were mine.

But I still couldn't figure the bumps. I could now type and write and dial and drive. I could hold flatware and read books—almost everything—but those bumps had me stymied. I finally broke down.

"Doctor, I can't figure these things out."

"But you're doing so well. What's the problem?"

"It's these rubber things."

He laughed.

"I thought maybe they were for opening bottles, or balancing a fork, or turning something, but they just don't make sense."

Why was he enjoying this?

"Mr. Showers, I have learned something about you."

"Huh?"

"Of course. It is obvious. You don't smoke."

Almost all prostheses are used by victims of war—unfortunate soldiers dismembered by some explosive or another. The state of the art in surrogate limbs had been designed for men most of whom smoked cigarettes. The bumps were to hold the cigarette butts.

"Well, I'll be—"

"That's all right Reverend Showers. That is the only mystery of these devices I am pleased you were unable to fathom. Now, tell me about this driving aid."

I did, with great pride. It had been another freedom, the victory of another adventure. It would collapse to fit in my brief case and it would work on any car or tractor steering wheel, including a go-cart.

My boys loved that. It was another in the many new projects we could share. I think I spent more time with them after the accident than before. They were all at an age where they needed their father around and I was in a place where I couldn't go far. It was a wonderful time of growth and togetherness.

They loved to watch me eat.

"Scott, don't eat with your fingers!"

"Why not? You do!"

"It's not the same."

"Oh?"

They wouldn't let me get away with anything.

Marilyn used to sit beside me at the table, cutting my meat and doing other things I had learned not to be too proud to ask of her. I started to rely on her, so she moved Michael in between us at the table. I was not to be served unduly, just loved.

After dinner the boys and I would roughhouse. I would take off my arms to avoid accident. They loved it. I no longer had as long a reach. I was at their mercy. Good for them. I was not some freak outsider who had invaded their house, someone to whom they had to show courteous respect. I was their dad and there were no holds barred. Good for me.

15

Inventions, adaptations, modifications—every day was a new test of resourcefulness. One of the church deacons liked to play golf, so I asked another friend, Ralph Anderson, to help me out. I didn't want to have to lug specialized clubs everywhere, so we invented clamps that made all clubs acceptable. I was never great at golf, but I was no worse now than I had been before the accident.

Bob Ybarra was to be my prosthetics man and a new and valuable friend. His mind and creativity would free me in so many ways.

Mark and the boys played baseball. A hasty twist of metal rods in a socket mount fit right on my wrist and right into a first baseman's mit. I was too old for the Dodgers, but I could still dream.

Chores around the ranch were similarly dealt with. A wrench and pliers were fitted to sockets, also a hammer and screwdriver. One day Larry and I were building the chicken coup. With a mighty swing he landed his hammer on an unprotected thumb. The ensuing language was not befitting a minister of God.

"Larry, watch your mouth."

"Well, for Pete's sake, I just smashed the h- - - outa my thumb."

"You don't see me crying, do you?"

I then proceeded to bash the beejeebers out of my left hook with my hammer attachment. I ducked in time to miss his unattached hammer, tossed mock-angrily at his unfair tormentor.

There were definite advantages to these strange contraptions, ungainly though they might seem. And they most decidedly did look ungainly, because I did not wear long-sleeve shirts. I was not ashamed of my hooks. I was, however, a little concerned about how others would view them.

Almost immediately after I got them I was to find out. Hope Baptist Church phoned. Now that I was out, would I resume the pulpit? I decided I would.

I was nervous. It had been a long time since I had faced a congregation. Would it be different? Would my changed circumstances change the way they accepted me? I caught my breath and walked out across the sanctuary. Everyone stood. Everyone was applauding—everyone, including two rows right in front of the pulpit that were filled with doctors and nurses and friends from the burn ward. So much, God has given me so much. They clapped and cried with laughter and joy. I just cried.

Shortly after that memorable first Sunday service I received a phone call from a reporter. I'm not sure how he heard about me, but he had been to the church that Sunday and felt there might be a story in my triumphant return. Could he have fifteen minutes? I agreed.

His name was Paul Dean. He was a pleasant man with an awkwardly professional attitude.

"Okay, now tell me a little about yourself, Reverend Showers."

I did. It didn't take long.

"Fine. Now tell me about your accident."

I did. I related the facts about the barn, the wire, seventy-two hundred volts.

"All right. Now, how did you feel about your welcome back to the church last Sunday?"

I told him I felt exalted, loved, tearful. I was brief.

Fifteen minutes had passed.

"Yes. Well, okay. Now is there anything that you haven't told me? Something the people might like to know?"

"Well, yes. But it probably wouldn't interest you."

He looked up from his pad. His eyes were like new hub caps, big and shining. I couldn't imagine what I had said, but the professional-stuck-with-a-human-interest-story boredom was completely gone.

"What did you leave out?" He was eager.

I told him.

"I had a kind of spiritual experience on the wire."

Somewhere between that sentence and his departure, two, then three hours flew by. He wanted to know everything. Who was there, who said what, when did it occur, what, how, why? For the first time since the accident it all came out. Even to Marilyn I hadn't revealed so much. When I had mentioned the vision to other ministers, it had been disregarded or passed off with an "Umm, very interesting." This man wanted to know.

The article came out the following Sunday. By Tuesday both the Associated Press and United Press International wire services had my story. So did every newspaper in the country, five magazines and eight foreign countries.

The dream was no longer a dream. Paul Dean's story brought in over twenty thousand dollars in less than six weeks. And people. And supplies. Paul Dean made the ranch finally real. Paul Dean was a miracle.

And the people began coming. One at a time or by the carful—a small family from the east or a busload from a church in California—as few as one and as many as a hundred. They came because of Paul Dean's story, because of the ranch, and because of me.

Rocks were moved, trenches were dug, fences were built. Pads were leveled. "What can we do?" "Can we help?" "We were in the neighborhood. Read about you in the paper. Need some help?" Some were friends; most were strangers.

Every so often a car would drive up and simply leave a

check, then drive on off to its original destination. There is no way to get to Rainbow Acres without going out of your way. All of them went out of their way, and all of them were glad they had.

A phone call came in from an old friend, Jim Soudriette.

"Ralph, I have a bunch of trees. Would you like to have them?"

A bunch of trees. Rainbow Acres was high desert scrub land. The barn was the tallest item in the place. I was the second tallest. To have a tree would be bountiful. A bunch of trees—wow!

"You bet we do!"

"Well, what kind to you need?"

"What kind do you have?"

"Oh I have some ash, some sugar maple, some mulberry. How many can you use?"

"How many? Uh . . ."

"How big a place do you have there?"

"About ten acres."

Then he started rattling off what he had for me. About fifty of these and forty of those. He had almost a hundred of another kind. I almost came unglued. This was what they meant when they talked about manna from heaven. He was talking about more than two hundred trees.

"Do you have a drill or something?"

"A drill?"

"Yes, an auger or something to plant these things, to dig holes with."

"You bet." I was going to get one that second.

"I'll be by with the trees in three days. Is that okay?"

"Perfect."

He hung up, and I had Larry on the phone in six seconds.

"Two hundred trees," I shouted. "Great big ones! You have to drill a hole to plant them. They'll be here in three days."

Now both of us were bouncing. We had no idea how much work it would take to drill two hundred holes.

We got a fence post drill and went to work. Three solid days of drilling. Two hundred holes, six feet deep by two feet wide. Rainbow Acres looked like twenty miles of chicken pox. We broke our backs, but the vision of two hundred trees kept us working.

"How big a truck does he have to haul that many trees?"

"I'll bet he uses C. A.'s truck. That big lowboy of his could do it if they're not too big."

"Two hundred trees. An instant forest. Just add water and dig."

We dug. Three days passed. The phone rang.

"Hi, this is Jim Soudriette. I have your trees. Can you meet me over at Middle Verde Road and I-17?"

"Sure." Oh boy, oh boy, oh boy!

I hopped into the truck and drove down to guide him up to the ranch. Visions of great green sugar plums danced in my head.

I got to the appointed spot. No trucks. An occasional car whizzed by, but no truck. A tiny little Japanese job came to a stop on the far side of the highway. But no trucks. I waited.

Then I saw this man come galloping across the freeway with a huge paper bag.

"Hi there, Ralph. Got your trees for you. I have to be on my way. Good luck now."

I sat there with my mouth open.

He tossed in the sack and galloped back across the freeway. I couldn't bring myself to look. The ranch looked like a gopher's picnic, and I was holding the bag. I looked.

Two hundred trees, all about twelve skinny inches long, stuffed bare-rooted into a Goodwill bag. I could have died. Larry was going to kill me. I sat there for an eternity. Maybe I should go to Europe. I drove home.

We stuck these bristly toothpicks into two hundred caverns. I was mortified. Larry was silent. We both looked up, looked at each other, and howled in laughter for the rest of the week. So much for big dreams.

Just as a point of information, almost every tree lived.

Almost every tree is over twenty feet high at this writing. So much for big dreams.

Most of the people who visited the ranch found my hooks interesting. They would come up to greet me and offer to shake my hand. I'd offer them a hook in return. Almost everybody took my hook and shook it like a hand. Occasionally, some people would put one hand on my shoulder and shake my hook with their other hand. One day a man came up and offered his hand; I offered my hook, and he smiled and hugged me. I liked that. I am by nature a toucher, but I never got the pleasure of touching my visitors when they took my hook. I liked it when they shared the touch by holding my arm. I loved it when that man hugged me. Now I hold my hook out a little wide in hopes that others will move in for a hug. A lot of people do.

Hugging was just another way I was learning how to cope with my new circumstances. Just as in driving and playing ball, I was getting daily more skillful at learning new ways to function normally. I still relied heavily on Marilyn for assistance, or on Larry or Joy, and even on the kids. I didn't like having to be helped, so I kept teaching myself more and more ways not to need it. Finally my big chance came to break away.

I was going to deliver a speech in Los Angeles, and I was going to go alone. Now I would see how capable I was.

I had had many earlier experiences with the general public, but this trip would be the clincher. My first sortie into the world beyond the ranch was a dinner given for me by the Verde Valley Rotary Club in Cottonwood.

It was to be my trial balloon. I was to eat at a table with people other than family, and I wanted to do it well.

I got to the restaurant early to make sure my food was cut up and a straw was provided in advance. Hooks are better made for grasping than for cutting and lifting. The dinner hour arrived and I sat straight in my chair at the head of the table. All the Rotarians filling the room had a direct view of me. I was a member of this club. They knew me; but all was new now.

I carefully opened a straw for my drink. Everybody watched. I tried to appear relaxed, so I talked to the men near me as I ate. Everybody watched. I would take a sip, lift my head to talk, take a bite, turn my head to answer, and on and on. Every time I lifted my head, everybody looked down at his plate. Every time I made a move downward to eat, everybody looked up to watch.

I was doing fine; they were tossing food all over the place. I'm a fast talker and a fast eater, so I was bobbing up and down like a fishing float. In their haste to avoid my seeing them stare, they were jerking and dodging and spilling glasses and dropping buttered rolls and food. It was a catastrophe.

I stood up. "Okay, everybody stop."

The room's eyes widened. What was I up to?

"You guys are making a terrible mess."

Roars of laughter.

"Now for the sake of your laundry bills, I am going to sit down and eat, never lifting my head up, and you guys just stare to your hearts' content. I promise I won't catch you, and you may even get a little dinner in you, not on you."

Applause.

I sat down and the meal continued splendidly.

I guess I will always have a problem with restaurants. But it's kind of fun. I'll sit and eat and bob up and down as I eat, and everyone else in the place gets whiplash. I finally decided that I had to slow down. I learned to make a broad I'm-coming-up-now gesture before lifting my head in order to allow my spectators a more graceful retreat. Everyone gets his view, which is fine with me, but a lot fewer Big Macs land on the floor.

I remember one unusual time, though. I was eating dinner with a family in Olean, New York—a little farm community I visited on a fund-raising journey. The daughter of my hosts, about sixteen or seventeen years old, sat kitty-corner from me at the table. After the prayer and about two minutes into the meal, she sat back, plopped her elbows on the table, and rested her chin in her hands. She looked squarely at me.

"Do you mind if I watch you eat?" she asked most sincerely.

It was just beautiful. I had never met anyone as straightforward as this girl. This was refreshing.

"You go right ahead."

And she did. She never took her eyes off me for the whole meal. Of course, nobody else does either, but she was so beautifully honest. I just smiled and ate.

So I had had a lot of experiences encountering society, but I had no experience and only minimal confidence in confronting society's obstacles for myself. All those barriers the unhandicapped world sets up unknowingly for the handicapped. All those doors and whatevers that are so unhard for normal people, but that are so un-easy for a man with no hands. This first trip to Los Angeles would break the ice, or me.

I packed my bags, stuck my steering wheel gadget in my briefcase, and headed down to Phoenix to catch my plane.

16

This was my maiden voyage. Being on the plane would be no problem; I would just sit there like everybody else. Getting to the plane and then getting off the plane and out of the terminal were the hurdles. Then there would be all the bother with strange rooms and unusual situations.

I was to drive myself to the airport, get on the plane, get off the plane, take care of my luggage, rent myself a car, drive to the motel, take care of all bodily needs, get to my appointed speech, go back to the motel, get to sleep, get up, get back in the car, get back to the plane, fly home, get my stuff, get to the truck, and drive to the ranch. What's so tough about that? What could go wrong? Surely I could do that. If I could do that I could do anything.

I wondered if I could do all this with nobody noticing I had unusual hands.

One of my earliest purchases of hardware was a pair of plastic, handlike attachments. They looked very real in a plastic kind of way. If people didn't look too closely, the attachments would go unnoticed.

I had acquired the hands to help me in my barbershop singing. Ever since high school I had been an avid barbershopper. I didn't want the audience to be upset with my armlessness, so I got these "hands" in order to enable them to enjoy the music. Barbershop tenors are always flailing away in broad, expressive gestures during songs, and I was one of the all-time great flailers.

117

Anyway, I went to this sing and my quartet came out on stage to much applause. There were at least five hundred people in the audience, very few of whom had ever even heard of me. It was a charity banquet and spirits were very high. We began to sing.

I have a habit of picking out individuals in the audience to sing directly to. It helps me get right into the fun of it. This night I started off with the person seated front table center as my initial point of focus. After only a few bars, I saw her turn to the person behind her and whisper. The second person then turned to a third and whispered something. The third turned to the fourth, the fourth to the fifth, and this was happening all along the long rows of tables. Finally, somewhere in each row, someone who knew me would smile and whisper back to the person before him, and the whole chain would reverse.

I knew they were talking about my hands. Were they real? Why did they shine like that in the lights? Finally somebody would know and tell everybody else. Nobody had any idea what we were singing. I vowed never to wear those things again.

Now, while we sing, I stand out there with bare hooks blazing. I gesture and wave and nobody cares. Sometimes in a comedy sing I'll release my back muscles and let the things just drop off and dangle. It's a built-in show-stopper that never fails to get a laugh.

But, this time there were no stage lights, and no broad gestures. This time I would wear the "hands" and nobody would know the difference. This time would be different.

I put on the "hands," a long-sleeved shirt and my suit coat. I drove to the airport and parked the truck. No problem. I got my ticket and boarded the plane. No one even looked up. Excellent. I left the plane and went to rent a car. The Hertz girl spotted me right off as I arranged the pen to sign the papers, but that was not really a problem. Things were going splendidly.

Somewhere between the Hertz booth and the baggage

claim area, I had accidentally bumped the hand and moved the wrist release switch to off. Not realizing this, I reached for my suitcase on the baggage turnstile and the hand dropped to the conveyer belt. Up to that second, everything was perfect, but now my seemingly perfect hand was traveling around the belt for all to see. It just continued going around and around as I tried to figure out how either to remove it or to hide under the floor tiles.

I could feel hot sweat trickling over my entire body. Every eye in the terminal was glued to this hand that was traveling around the baggage area. I just stepped back a little and planned on a quick grab on its next circumnavigation, followed by a hasty retreat to the nearest hole. Everybody was dying in painful embarrassment. This was awful. I was six inches high and melting. Nobody moved. The air was like a sauna bath.

Out of nowhere, a tiny old lady edged up to the belt. She stood between me and the whole wide world and said in a voice that almost drowned out the public address system:

"Sonny, it looks like you could use a hand."

I doubt that she had intended the pun, but it was perfect. The entire gathered population of the world, horror-struck the second before, broke apart. First a chuckle, then spontaneous gales of laughter. My life was spared.

"Yes, ma'am, I sure could."

Off she went, like an aged shot, around the turnstile. The belt was only barely slower than she. She chased that silly chunk of plastic three quarters of the way around the room, scooting in front of the amassed howling multitudes, until she caught up with it. All the while she was calling, "Hand, hand, hold still now." If I hadn't been laughing as hard as everybody else, I would have rolled myself up in a ball and crawled into a hole.

"I got it! Here it is!"

Back she came, and with arthritic hands she attempted to replace my fallen appendage. She was working like a saint, and I was blushing like a school girl.

Her husband came up. He was the only person west of New York who hadn't witnessed this spectacle. What he saw was his wife trying to push a hand onto a stranger.

"Honey, what are you doing?"

"Putting his hand back on."

I should have charged admission. This show was worth twenty dollars anywhere. We were no longer in an airline terminal, we were center stage at the Met.

The old man just turned and walked away. He had no idea who this lady was; he was a vision of nonchalance. Jack Benny would have traded his Maxwell for this show.

Properly rehanded, I picked up my bags, thanked her for her kindness, and slunk away into hoped-for oblivion. All I can say for myself was that I didn't bolt and run. I was the picture of calm. Nothing out of the ordinary had happened. But my heart felt like a popcorn popper gone amuck.

No further incidents occurred during the remainder of the day. I got to my room unnoticed by all but the desk clerk, who saw me sign the register.

The speech I'd come to Los Angeles to deliver went off without a hitch, and I slept like a log that night. I checked out with grace and headed back to the airport.

I had to go to the bathroom.

My prostheses were not really good at getting my belt taken care of. Today was especially hard; the buckle was caught. I was in the men's room, just off the pot, and I was stuck. What could I do? Marilyn wasn't there to put me back together. Decision time.

"Well, Ralph, you better grab yourself by the tail and get this thing done."

I held up my pants as best I could and went to stand outside the bathroom door. I was going to ask the first man who came by to help me. I was ready for the worst.

"Excuse me, sir, could you help me?"

"Pardon me?"

"I can't get my belt hooked up. You see, it's stuck, and I have no hands. Could you help me?"

"Sure, glad to. No problem."

He got me all zipped up right there in the lobby.

"Thank you. I really appreciate that."

"Hey, we handicapped have got to stick together."

He looked fine to me.

"What's your handicap?"

"I have cancer. I'm going to die in the next six months."

And he walked off. We were just passing experiences in each other's lives.

17

Everything seemed to be timed perfectly for all the disorienting jumble of crises, blessings, situations, and complications. If it hadn't been for that disastrous meeting of the Buena Park Church's Board of Trustees, Marilyn and I wouldn't have left for Arizona. If we had had more money, we would certainly have stayed in Wickenburg and might never have found Camp Verde. The bank had turned us down and the Browns had come to our rescue with a rainbow-tiered plot of hills. We needed jobs and the telephone rang. Larry was ready to start his ministry at that perfect time in his life when what I had to offer was what he needed.

And then there was the accident. My wonderful barn and the high, but not high enough, power lines.

And then there was God.

When I arrived in the Verde Valley I had great pity for the handicapped. Now I was handicapped, and I could understand. Now we could work together.

In the long weeks in the hospital, my past and present had begun to make sense with my future. I had doubted; I had been afraid. But God's promise and Marilyn's love had brought me through.

Timing.

There was Mr. Dean's article coming out just as we were ready to plunge back into the ranch. The newswire services grabbing up his story and ricocheting it all over the world.

How many of the daily hundreds of human interest stories that emerge from the little newspapers of the world get so magnificently broadcast to a loving, caring world so often accused of indifference?

Timing, miraculous timing.

The people came in droves to help. They offered to build stairs for our mobile home and to add a porch. People, families, children, buses, cars, and letters—everything converged at the exact time of our need.

And then there was the water system problem. Have you ever tried to get a license from a state that required a license, but had none to offer? That lovely white pebble that Larry and I had tossed onto our alkaline desert paradise had given us more water than we could use. The state insisted we lay out a water system to divert the precious water to the various building sites on the property. The building sites were determined by the tossing of more white stones.

An engineer volunteered to design the system for free. We told him what we wanted; the state told him what we had to have; and by the time all the involved participants out in left field had added their special stipulations, he came up with a water system. It was such a hugely complicated project it would cost fifteen thousand dollars.

We were barely open; we didn't even have a rancher in residence; and we had to come up with fifteen thousand dollars. Where in the world were we going to find fifteen thousand dollars?

Timing.

The bill came in. Mr. Dean's story went out. The money rolled in. Water, water, everywhere.

And the mail kept coming. Enough money to do all the little projects that were needed to prepare for Rainbow Acres. And the people kept coming. Enough to clear pads, move rocks, and generally prepare for Rainbow Acres. We weren't ready to really get the ranch off the ground, but we could begin to see the light.

Another letter arrived. It was from Ewa Beach, Hawaii. It

started: "Dear Ralph, please come to see us. Tickets enclosed."

The young people from the Ewa Beach Baptist Youth Fellowship had held car washes, cake sales, and other fund raisers to earn the money to bring the Showerses back for a visit and a rest. It was all happening so fast—the arms, the ranch, everything—that a rest was exactly what I needed, and it came just when I needed it.

Timing.

It was good to meet our friends again—to see how the church had grown, changed, stayed the same. We met new people and were sad to have missed old friends. Our joy was only dampened by the knowledge that we had left trouble brewing back at the ranch.

The trouble had all started during my last weeks in the hospital. Marilyn had told me and an old friend, Bill Beamon, about the man from Arizona Public Services who had come to measure the barn. She also mentioned how the APS had started pulling up and repositioning some of the telephone poles in the area. Then she mentioned that a representative from the service had dropped by shortly before we went to Hawaii to offer us financial assistance if they could.

All this confirmed in my head the fact that I was in for deep trouble. I had destroyed the entire phone and power system. They had measured the barn and probably knew I had no permit to haul so large an object on the roadways. This was going to be a tough one.

"Something smells funny here." Bill had looked puzzled. We had been in the ministry together before he resigned and started his new business. This had been the insurance man part of him speaking.

"Let it alone, Bill," I had said. "I don't want to get socked with a suit for destroying property."

"No—there's something odd here. They did something wrong. The APS doesn't go around ta-ta-ing to people they're going to sue. They're worried about something. You ought to talk with your lawyer."

I had done so, more to make sure I was safe than anything else.

Bill Harrell, the man who helped us put together the corporation papers for the ranch, had come by the hospital to see what it was that was worrying me. I related the whole story, complete with descriptive fears of a thousand disconnected phone calls.

"This stinks." I had heard that phrase before, put less bluntly. Mr. Harrell was normally very professional, but he had seemed to drop some of his cool exterior. "We're going to need some help with this one. The part about no permit for the barn is sticky, but why did they move those poles so fast?"

After that my brother Jim got into the act. This was starting to get out of hand.

Pretty soon we had one of the top lawyers in the state on board. I was getting worried. The process was becoming too complex. They were talking about thousands of dollars. I was glad to have gotten out without being sued. They were talking about low wires and high voltage, while I was simply glad to be alive.

Numbers started being thrown around. Ten thousand dollars, maybe more. My share would be enough to help pay off the final hospital bills. On the whole, I wished they would just drop the whole thing. As far as I was concerned, I had come out ahead already.

This continued through those rough first weeks out of the hospital. The big-city lawyer was going to draw up a preliminary letter simply stating what had happened and asking the Arizona Public Service people what they were going to do. All this legal business had me ready for a vacation when the letter came from the Ewa Beach young people. But even in Hawaii, surrounded by its beauty and the generous love of my friends, I was having a tough time getting it out of my brain.

The lawyer had said the letter ought to get things moving. I wasn't too sure which way the moving things would turn. The passing of time and the spell of the blue-water

beaches eventually dulled my worries. I was finally starting
to relax when the phone call came in.

It was Bill Harrell. His voice was sharp and businesslike,
giving nothing away by inflection.

"Ralph."

"Yes, sir."

"I just got a call from Rosengren." That was the big-city
lawyer. "Four lawyers from New York City just came by his
office. They wanted to discuss your case."

"And?" I was never one for terrific questions, but this
man was not helping my nerves one bit.

"They simply sat down and asked if you would accept
three hundred twenty-five thousand dollars with no
questions."

"Three hundred twenty-five thousand dollars?"

"Yes. I think we've got something here."

I was jumping up and down like a Calaveras County frog.

"Three hundred twenty-five thousand dollars?"

"I think they would probably settle for a million."

"I don't need a million."

"Excuse me?" I had startled him.

"I don't need that much. My share of all that money is
more than enough."

"Oh, Ralph, I think you're wrong. We can—"

"No, we can't! I'm just thankful for the $325,000. I can
build the whole ranch right now with that money."

I was a kid of ten. I was bouncing like a ball and hollering
for Marilyn to come hear the news. We were rich. The
ranch was rich.

"Ralph, we, you—"

"Thank you very much. Just tell the men that I must be
about God's work. I'll see you in a week."

I hung up. I'm sure he stared at his receiver for ten
minutes, but I was happy. Happy? I was beside myself.

The Goehners and Showerses had projected a seven-year
growth pattern. We would be open by the summer.

Two hundred seventy-five thousand dollars. That was to

be our share after the lawyers got their cut. Man, what we could do with all that money. We could use it as collateral or spend it on anything. We could make loans, give gifts—just about anything.

The first thing we did was take ten percent off the top and give it away. We gave it to churches and other projects we liked, and to friends who wanted to adopt children. I think the most fun I've ever had was giving away that money.

No strings attached. You're my friend; have some cash. Marilyn and I really loved giving that money away. What's the point of having a new toy if you can't share it with your friends?

What a trip. What a place to be happy. Ewa Beach, Hawaii, surrounded by friends and loved ones. But I still couldn't wait to get back to the ranch.

18

We had the money, we had the land, we had the desire, and we had no idea it would all come together so quickly. We had to get busy. Miracles abounded and we were bound by them.

Again I thought to myself, all this is too much for coincidence. We have been charged to do something very special and we had better get to it.

Double-wide mobile homes were ordered for living quarters. Master architectural plans were devised, changed, and altered. The water system was completed. The future loomed before us, and we were thrilled.

The plan was for the creation of a ranch for mentally retarded young men, living in groups of six to a home. We dropped this to four when the Navy donated beds and chests of drawers, which, when set in place, left no room for Ranchers. Each unit would be supervised by two houseparents who would also live in the home. Creative, but profitable, work projects would be devised in order to provide as close to normal a living style as possible. Everything would be set up to enable the Ranchers to grow to their fullest potential.

The inhabitants would be called Ranchers, not clients or patients. This was to be their home, their ranch. To be a rancher in America is to be rich, and we would be rich in life and hope. We would not be just another institution.

There would be no church or chapel on the premises.

The Ranchers would come from many different backgrounds. No one would be forced to be Baptist simply because the Goehners and Showerses were. Besides, going to church is not going across the lawn. It is the whole act of preparing and going into town for a special occasion. It is something one does because one wants to, not because one has to. If a Rancher did not choose to attend church at all he would not be made to.

There would be no resident doctor. The Ranchers would be introduced to several available doctors, dentists, psychiatrists, and clinics. Then they would make their own choice within the scope of their finances, just like everyone else.

At one point, during an onsite visit prior to opening day, the state tried to force us into having a resident psychiatrist or psychologist at the ranch. The inspector was busy doing his job, thoroughly, tediously, reading down his checklist of requirements.

"Where is your psychiatrist?"

"He is in Cottonwood." Knowing where this was going, I became a little apprehensive.

"Why is he in Cottonwood?"

"That's where he lives. He has his practice in Cottonwood."

The inspector was beginning to look concerned. This was not as his book said it should be.

"Why doesn't he live here?"

"Do you have a psychiatrist living in your house?"

"Well, no."

"How come?"

"Well, I could never afford one."

"Praise the Lord, neither can we."

There followed a short pause and then a long chuckle. This may have been our first and only human being in government dress.

"I see what you mean. What do we look at next?"

Another miracle—a government with a heart.

In all decisions about how life should be at the ranch, we

always asked each other what normal people would do. After all, we were all normal people on the whole who happen to be handicapped in different ways. And isn't that true of the world? Everybody has a handicap. Some people are slow; some have insides that don't work too well; some have bad hearts or legs or eyes. Everybody has a handicap, but it's how each person uses those handicaps, how he or she lives with and beyond them that makes each one individual, special. And we were all to be special.

The ranch was to be home, not a summer camp or short-term institution. A Rancher would be welcome to live his whole life at Rainbow Acres. During his younger working years, he would live with his ranch family. When he grew too old or too ill to continue the daily routine, he would be allowed to move into a retirement home right on the ranch—not as excess baggage, but as an active senior citizen within the community. Finally, for the later years, a rest-home facility would be available for those too old or disabled to manage on their own. All of these services would be conducted within the framework of the expanded, loving family. And all of these services would be equally available to staff members.

Great dreams, great plans. But now it was up to us to carry them out. We had the plan and the plant. Now we needed the people. First of all we needed houseparents.

I had gotten out of the hospital in December. In January, Mr. Dean had written his article with the resultant flood of people and aid.

Marilyn and I returned from Ewa Beach in February and started the actual building of the ranch during March, April and May. We wanted to open June 1, one year to the day from our first coming to Arizona, but we couldn't find anyone to work as houseparents. In Ewa Beach we had become acquainted with some people who thought they would like to work during the summer, but were unable to come now. Nobody seemed interested.

We placed ads in all the papers and posted notices in all the area churches. We mailed out requests to friends and asked them to ask other friends. We were frantic. We were getting nowhere. We were begging people to work with us. Nothing.

One night in early May, Marilyn sat us all down at the table. Her voice was not angry, but firm.

"You are doing this all wrong!" It was an admonition.

"What are we doing wrong?" I was a little defensive. We had done everything we could think of and some things that other people thought of.

"You built this ranch on faith. God gave all this to you. All you ever had to do was ask Him."

"Right, but—" We were startled. Larry and I were always spouting off about God this and God that.

"Well, have you asked the Lord for houseparents?"

Larry and I were always so accustomed to having everything set down before us that we sometimes forgot who was the Provider. It all seemed so simplistic: pray and jobs materialize; pray and wells spring forth. It was a little unnerving. Marilyn was right. We had failed to ask God's help.

All four of us went back to our knees. Larry said he would take all the ads out of the papers. If God wanted us to have houseparents, He would provide them.

The next day Larry and I drove down to Mesa where we were to meet and interview a potential Rancher. We wanted to start with a full home, and at that time only Mr. and Mrs. Yeatman's son Ronnie was scheduled to move in. This was to be another Ronnie, only he went by the nickname Bimbo.

Bimbo was perfect. He was a pleasant, outspoken young man with a real zest for life. We approved him on the spot and explained to Mrs. Needham, his mother, that he could move up as soon as we found a qualified houseparent to supervise the home. Then we left.

Before we reached the car Pat Needham ran out of the house to stop us. She was excited, but looked worried about what she was going to ask.

"I know this is going to sound strange, but, well, could I be a houseparent?"

She was a single woman, experienced with living around

a retarded adult, filled with love and needing a job. Thank
you, Lord. Now we had a ranch, a houseparent and two
Ranchers, both named Ronnie. We would open by the first
of June.

Then we interviewed L. C. Coleman, a young black man
who had been placed in a boarding house by the correctional department. He was quiet, withdrawn, and sometimes sullen, and most of all he seemed especially to need
us. We fell in love with him, and that made three.

Rancher number four came from nearby Prescott, Arizona. His name was George Leichty.

These then were our first-born, our first Ranchers:
Ronald "Bimbo" Cadman, Ronald Yeatman, L. C. Coleman, and George Leichty. Pat Needham, Bimbo's mother,
was our housemother, and Rainbow Acres was ready to
open.

Others were to follow, like a gathering of eagles. Susan
Barrett had been interested in us for a long time, but wasn't
sure how she could help. Besides, we had no money to pay
her. We talked about her being a houseparent, but we kept
coming back to how Larry and I needed help with the running of the ranch. Finally, after much searching of her soul,
she came to us happily to take over the administrative work
for very little money, a place to stay, and our promise that
she wouldn't starve.

We needed a ranch foreman, and Jim Bowser and family
were asked to come. With two master's degrees, this high-
school teacher with a wife and five children of his own had
been a friend in Ewa Beach. He was looking for a job back
on the mainland, and he loved kids. Three hundred dollars
a month plus basics is not very tempting to most men with
large families. The Bowsers' hearts were bigger than their
budgets, and they came to join the eagles at Rainbow Acres.

A TV interview found our next eagles. A retired couple
from Phoenix, Mr. and Mrs. E. G. Young, wrote and asked
if they could join us in God's work. They were to be our
second houseparents.

We have made many mistakes along the way, mostly because we failed to let God in on what we were up to. Now when things seem to be rolling along well, we think of Marilyn's challenge to us to turn our problems over to God. From a house with no dwellers, our prayers and trust found us with a ranch gathered with eagles. On June 1, 1974, Rainbow Acres was a reality. By the end of July we would swing open our doors to let the world see what we had done.

First, there was a lot of work to be done, and all of us were going to pitch in and do it.

19

So now the real work was to begin. Now we were all to find out if prayers and aspirations combined with love could actually create a working ranch for retarded adults. We had talked for so long, but we had never actually done this thing before. All of us had spent time with retarded and handicapped people, but none of us had ever tried living twenty-four hours a day in such an environment. In our hearts we knew we could do it. In reality we were a little anxious.

The ranch was open. The end of July was to be Open House. We had received some hesitation from members of the Camp Verde community about having these retarded people in their midst. We wanted to put forward a strong image of normalcy and self-sufficiency at the Open House.

So much work had been done for us by volunteers and friends, that the ranch had a moving-toward-completion look from the first. We wanted to get some of the final rough edges cleaned up before the spectators came.

After a day of acclimating the Ranchers to their new home, Larry and I set up a series of work projects that would have the place ready for tourists. Large white rocks were moved into place to form walkways and roadsides. Scrub brush was cleared, and a huge garden plot was outlined in preparation for planting. We had over a month to get things growing, if we got right on it. The garden could stand as a symbol of permanence before Open House.

First a trench had to be dug to bring in water for the garden. Then long furrows had to be cut for the rows of corn and vegetables. This was hard work and time-consuming, but relatively easy. Now came time for planting. We were going to start with corn.

L. C., Ronnie, George, and Bimbo stood at one end of the first long furrow, packages of corn seed in hand, ready to work. Larry and I had some other work to do on a fence that we were putting around the ranch, so we were going to turn the men loose on the planting by themselves.

Larry gave them their instructions. First you dig a little hole, then you drop in the seed, then you cover it up and add a little water. As he explained, he demonstrated. There seemed to be no problem. All right, then; plant corn.

They did. George got down and dug the hole. Ronnie hit it with his foot. L. C. started digging in the dirt with both hands and Bimbo poured the entire package of seed on top of the mess.

Larry looked over at me. Here we were, the great saviors of the mentally retarded. We both just shook our heads. What we had here was the most tightly condensed corn field in history. An entire field on a postage stamp. The fence would have to wait; we had to become teachers.

We progressed step by step. "Dig the hole." Everybody learned to dig a hole. "Plant three seeds in the hole." All four dumped their whole package of seeds into the hole. Then we realized these men didn't know how to count. We had to teach them.

Squatting down in the middle of the future field, Larry and I taught basic counting. One, two, three. Finally everybody could count to ten and planting began again. Almost every hole got three seeds, but one hole was here, another was over there and the third got lost in the dirt from the fourth. We had to teach them how to measure.

Relative distances are not important to people who have never had to deal with them. Two sticks were broken, one at approximately twelve inches, and the other, three inches long. The holes were to be one long stick apart from each other and one short stick deep.

A lot of time was spent on all these lessons, and attention spans varied greatly among the four Ranchers; but they all truly wanted to do it right, so they listened. They fidgeted, they looked up at the powder-blue sky and watched the ravens or the clouds, but mostly they listened.

We knew we couldn't ask them to absorb much more that day. We weren't sure we had much more to give, so we turned them loose again. Eager to please and eager to play, these four men tore up that field. Lay down stick, dig hole, stick in stick, drop in one, two, three seeds, cover up hole, pat down, water, lay down stick. The neatly plowed furrows looked like a battle zone, but the seeds were in. Later, as the corn began to sprout and grow, the effect of the planting was apparent. The organization was a disaster, but the corn was growing and, my, what a beautiful sight it was!

That night Joy and Larry joined Marilyn and me on the porch of our mobile home. We laughed and cried and cried and laughed and generally realized that we had painted ourselves straight into a corner. We had no way out. We were stuck, and we loved it. It was a magnificent unforgettable night. We knew we could make it. We had taught, we had worked, we had loved. We looked forward to tomorrow.

The four Ranchers were as different as any four humans can be. Any thought of stereotyping retarded people into neatly organized groups of learning patterns and personality traits is as ridiculous as trying to lump any four other "normal" people into categories. The only thing these four men had in common was their desire to learn.

I have always objected to the classifications that researchers and grant-funded educators have come up with for retarded people, from the early brands like *moron* and *idiot* to the modern expressions like *developmentally disabled*. Mentally retarded people are just that, mentally retarded. Retarded means slowed, not stopped. Only in the case of the severely or profoundly retarded does it seem unlikely that they will want to learn. Almost all programs for retarded carry them up to their eighteenth year. From there on out they and their parents largely have to fend for themselves. I believe that at age eighteen the retarded finally start to want to learn. Their development is such that now they are ready to grow.

All four of our first Ranchers were testimony to that. It took hard work, patience, and love, but the rewards to those of us who cared were incredible. Every day we witnessed the joyous blossom of another idea, skill, or confidence.

George was a perfect example. He walked like a robot and stuttered interminably. His bright red hair was constantly tousled as he worked through the frustrations of getting out a sentence. His lock-kneed gate made him a sure bet to trip over anything. He was constantly falling down the stairs going into Apache House, as we had named the first mobile home.

One day everybody was gathering behind Apache for a pot luck. All hands were pitching in—cooking, setting up, carrying food to the tables. Housemother Pat Needham was scurrying all over the kitchen handing out chores and setting up dishes. In her hurry, she thrust a plate of stuffed tomatoes at George and asked him to take them down to the table.

Obliging as ever, George took the plate and headed toward the stairs. Pat instantly realized that this could only result in catastrophe, but the die was cast. She could not shame him by retrieving the plate, so she just sat down and awaited the inevitable.

A picture of George face down in stuffed tomatoes filled her brain. Her ears rushed with the as-yet-unheard sounds of crashing platter and body. She heard his shuffling steps descending the stairs. She was taut, alert, ready to spring to his rescue, powerless to prevent the coming disaster.

"M-m-mother—d-don't worry. I m-m-made it." It was George's thrill-filled voice. He had known what she had expected. He had expected it too, but he had made it and the world was beautiful.

Pat held back her emotion as she called down, "That's good, George. Put it on the table and come back. I have more things for you to carry."

George was also famous for moving to within two inches of a person's face if he wanted to talk to him. This could be very disconcerting. Marilyn and Joy finally set down the law on that point. If George wanted to talk to them he had to stand at least two feet away. At first they would physically position him at the proper distance. Then they reminded him; then they just expected him to follow through. He did.

Ronnie Yeatman was another one for closeness. He loved to hug. It didn't matter who or where, Ronnie would move his husky blond body right into a person and lay on a bear hug—friends and total strangers alike. More often than not, this was embarrassing, but Ronnie couldn't be stopped.

We spent many hours trying to explain to him that some behavior just wasn't appropriate. We tried everything we could think of to break him from the habit. Finally at a fund-raising event at Knott's Berry Farm in California, Ronnie put the hug on one too many people. We were at a gas station just outside the amusement park. A woman drove up to get gas and got out of her car. Ronnie made a beeline right toward her, arms spread wide for the clutch and a grin spread all over his face. That woman took her purse and belted him over the head with it.

Ronnie just stood there, arms still spread, but the grin was changed to total confusion. Slowly his arms fell and he turned to me.

"Is that what you mean?" he asked sheepishly.

"That's what I mean."

The lesson wasn't complete, but that well-placed hand-bag was the necessary breakthrough. I laughed till I almost fell over, and gave Ronnie the biggest hug he ever had.

George and Ronnie were a constant source of merriment to us all. The antics they could devise would keep us in stitches for hours. I remember the contest with the trees. We had bunches of those tiny twelve-inch trees left over from the famous tree-gift fiasco, and Ronnie and George were going to finish planting them.

Sometimes George would just refuse to work. Once while we were setting up a rock garden during a hot summer afternoon, he stood erect, planted his feet apart, put his hands on his hips, and announced he wasn't going to do any more. He just stood there, riveted, his mind made up. Finally we gave up on him, finished the garden, and went in. He stayed fixed for twenty more minutes before he joined us for iced tea. We learned we had to be creative to get him to work.

Ronnie was always a good worker. Give him a job, some explanation, and supervision, and he would plug away till it was done. Both men liked candy bars.

A contest was arranged in order to get the trees planted. The holes were all dug, but there was no water near the planting areas. Ronnie was to set in the little trees, fill the dirt, and pat them down as George hurried over to the far house pad, got a bucket of water, and returned to pour it on the hole. I was to holler "go," and the first one done got a point toward the candy bar. This was the contest. Everything was set.

"Go!" I yelled as George and Ronnie thrust themselves into their duties.

Ronnie started filling and George started running his duck-like, stiff-legged hobble after the water. It was neck and neck through the filling of the bucket. Then George rounded the fence on his home stretch.

At the top of his happy voice he called out, "Hey, C-C-C-Culligan m-m-m-man" and tripped on a rock. The word *m-m-m-man* was said in full horizontal flight. George came down with a splash, a splat, and a bloody nose. After two beats he looked up at me and said, "I d-d-d-didn't do that t-t-t-t-too well."

Here we were, three handicapped men, laughing aloud

at one of our misfortunes. It was beautiful. Nobody's feelings were hurt. Everybody could appreciate the situation.

Another time, the wood-shop supervisor had given Eugene a piece of sandpaper to finish off some woodwork. He showed Eugene what to do and then left for a minute. When the supervisor came back, Eugene had turned the paper over so that he was sanding with the back. Or, rather, he wasn't sanding. John, the supervisor, turned the paper over and left again. When he returned the same thing had happened. This went on for ten minutes until John couldn't handle it any more and he left to talk to me.

As I approached the shop, Ronnie was standing outside.

"I helped Eugene with the sandpaper," he announced proudly.

John and I looked at each other and went inside. There sat Eugene sanding away with his paper folded in half. He was getting his work done and able to feel the rough surface of the paper at the same time. Ronnie had known what to do.

We would all help each other. Life was wonderful.

L. C. Coleman was actually the first Rancher to check in at Rainbow Acres. He was a thin black man of about five feet eight or so, with a loving smile and a hesitancy in his speech. He was also the first to leave us.

Such a happy young man, he loved us as we loved him. But there were other problems working against L. C. As with the rest of the world, there are some retardates who are also emotionally disturbed. L. C. was among those; he was a pyromaniac. The people at the probation department had not informed us of this, feeling his past incidents were isolated occurrences.

We were in the process of building the recreation hall, our first permanent structure. The day we put up the plaster wallboard, L. C. set fire to a cabinet. Had it not been for the new plasterboard, the whole building would have burned down.

We were stunned. L. C. was a loving young man who had

given us no clue of this problem. We knew he was a city dweller at heart, because he kept telling us how he missed the cars. Well, his fire brought cars and firetrucks up to the ranch in a hurry. Unfortunately, one of the cars was the probation officer, who took L. C. away.

We were down. We felt helpless, as though we had failed. It has never been easy for us to lose a member of our family, especially when the departure is so wrenching, as with L. C.

Bimbo, of course, was Pat Needham's son. He was a gentle giant at over six foot two and built like the proverbial brick outhouse. He was the muscle. It was Bimbo who built the ranch. He could lift anything and do everything. He may have been retarded, but he was by no means physically impaired.

My sons became very close to Bimbo. He was always up at our home tossing the baseball or shooting baskets with Mark and Scott. While we were setting up our third house, to be named Yavapai, Bimbo hit a line drive home-run through the front window.

Pat would discipline him equally with the other men, but silently prayed this hulk of a son of hers never got upset about the beratings. In fact, Bimbo never seemed to get upset about anything. He had the most joyous personality of any Rancher, then or since. It was a pleasure to be in his company, except when he got his motor mouth in gear— which was often—or when he went to work on his drum set, which was too often at twice a month.

Around September, Pat married the man she had been seeing for the past long while, and we had ourselves a full-time shop worker. Sadly for the ranch, by December, Pat's husband decided to leave the area and took his family with him. It was a great joy for us that they found happiness, but a great sorrow to see them leave.

But the ranch would survive. New Ranchers were waiting in line to join us, and new houseparents were beginning to come to our nest. Rainbow Acres was on its way, and our prize was about to join us.

20

Open House day came, bringing with it many dozens of curious friends and townspeople. What exactly was all this to-do up off of Middle Verde Road? By this time everybody knew a little bit or more about me. I was the preacher that got burned on the wire. I was the guy that the papers had talked about, the one who was going to bring all those retarded people into the area.

A lot of the townspeople knew Larry. He was the preacher over at the Indian Mission. Larry Goehner was the man who had been all over town enlisting help and acquiring ranch equipment. Somehow he and I were involved in this handicapped or retarded or whatever deal.

But what was all this about Rainbow Acres? This was mighty curious.

Of course many of the guests at the Open House were well aware of what was happening. They were friends or associates like Ray Smith and C. A. McDonald who had pitched in when the need was there. Some had donated money, others had given time, and all had prayed for us, though some were not entirely sure what they were praying for.

The ranch was beautiful. At least it was to us. Four double-wide mobile homes were assembled and in place. Two were residences; one was for Marilyn, the kids and myself; and one was for the Goehners. One more double wide was on the ranch, still separated from its other half and awaiting exact placement. And the barn was there. The barn. Everybody knew about the barn.

Roadways and walking paths were clearly defined by white-rock edging. Some fencing was up and more was obviously in progress. A strangely laid-out garden sat squarely in the middle of everything.

And then there were these four young men. They looked all right, but they were definitely different. The one man kept hugging everybody.

The visitors were attentive. They listened to what we had to say and some even asked questions. We told them of our dream, of our plans, of how they could help. Most left pleased, others left confused, and some were going to need some attention. The ranch was all right, maybe. Larry and I agreed that it wasn't enough to bring the town to us for approval. We were going to have to seek their respect actively. How would we do that?

This problem had to be set aside temporarily, put to the back of our minds as a nagging problem. There were other, more immediate situations to deal with. The second house was ready and the Youngs were ready to move in. We had to fill that house and get busy on the next before we could spend adequate time on the town problem.

Jeff Pitts had come in to fill the vacancy left by L. C.'s removal. Athletic like Bimbo, he was shy and very stand-offish. He had a passion for his motorcycle and a deep desire to return home. But, still, he was a loving addition to the ranch. Things would be very hard for him down the road. Both of his parents and his only sister would pass away during his early stay with us. It was a sad way to know that Jeff would be one of our life-long residents.

Then came the letter from Ripon, California. It was from a Mr. and Mrs. Van Dyken, who had heard about our ranch from the newspapers. They had a son who might fit into our program. Please send information. We did.

This was followed by more letters and phone calls.

Their son's name was David. The victim of cerebral palsy,

he had spent most of his life in a hospital bed, and was diagnosed as severely retarded.

It had never been our plan to include the severely retarded at the ranch. We did not have the facilities nor the expertise to deal with these people. But something in the way the Van Dykens described him, something in the sorrow that tinted their voices, plus some other unseen and unspoken force that seemed to surround our talks about David, made Larry and me decide to take a chance.

Larry flew up and joined the Van Dykens to visit David. For the first time, Larry witnessed in-depth a mental institution. What he saw shook him to his soul. The desperately ill, the discarded, the empty bodies that lived only in their heartbeats, lay or wandered around this sterile, protective prison. And then he saw David.

That really was all that could be said. He saw a human body, lying alive but vacant on a tight-sheeted bed. The body could not talk and had little if any control of his bodily movements.

Larry came home the next day, brokenhearted and saddened. We sat on the porch of his home and he told me what he had seen. He had felt so totally helpless. And he couldn't get David out of his mind. Describing that emaciated form who could not hear or talk and was physically incapable of much, Larry sat there and cried.

"But, Ralph," the tears choked his speech, "we have to try. There was something in his eyes. We have to try."

"Larry, you're the director here. You call the shots on this." I tried to sound professional, but I felt that God was in this case. I was so proud of Larry for his love and so thankful to God for this terrible opportunity. I knew that this was meant to be.

During this period of correspondence and visitations, the second house had filled up. Four men, ranging in age from eighteen to forty had joined our family. These were John, Ted, David B., and Tom—all of them wonderful people with much to offer and much to gain by their residency. All had stories that could fill a book, but it will have to be another book. It is enough to say that they all became integral members of the ranch and have found deep homes in our hearts.

There was no room for David Van Dyken. A third house, Hopi, had been erected. It was furnished and ready for occupancy, but there were no houseparents.

Roberta Patrick and Ellie Nakano had expressed an interest in working at the ranch for a summer. Teachers in Hawaii, they had heard me speak while Marilyn and I were back visiting our friends during our rest break in Ewa Beach. Would they be willing to come now and be houseparents as well as set up the special education project? Yes, they would. They came to spend a short time with us; they have stayed to build a ranch with us. David would have a home.

But could we help him?

Larry had noticed that David wore a hearing aid in his right ear. It did not seem to be helping him. A glance through his medical chart provided the reason why. The hearing aid was for his left ear. How long had that boy lain in bed, deaf to the world because of an oversight? We bought another hearing aid and fitted it to his left ear, leaving the misplaced aid to offer any assistance it might.

"David."

Long years of isolation were shattered with that word. His eyes lighted up. Awareness filled his face. A huge, toothy, wide-mouth grin joined his ears. He was no vegetable. He was alive and we could help him. The disinterest of the soundless void left him. He was alert. Was he retarded? Yes, but by birth, accident, or years of professional neglect, that we couldn't say.

This tall, blond, gangly person who could hardly walk and couldn't have cared less about the world around him, was alive. And he did learn to care. His parents were jubilant, we were jubilant and David was jubilant.

I went to meet David at the airport the day he came to live

with us. What a pair we made as I escorted him down the gangway from the plane. There I was at 5′ 8″ with shiny silver hooks alongside David, 6′ 4″ and flailing in the wind. I was very proud. The handicapped were helping the handicapped. We went to a pizza restaurant once and had the whole place in tears of laughter. Not laughing at us entirely, but with us.

We forced David to talk with us. If he wanted something he had to learn the words and articulate them. This took patience and love on all sides, because of the difficulty in understanding exactly what it was he was trying to say. But patience is a commodity that we have in abundance.

Now David walks, talks, does skilled work with his hands and is one of the best horsemen at the ranch. He fell off a lot at first, as he had great difficulty mounting and dismounting, but trial, error, and a deep desire to accomplish brought him through.

David is our prize. Recently he went through an operation to place a tiny electrode in the back of his head that should help him coordinate his motor/muscular skills. The future looks very bright for this "hopeless" young man from the mental institution.

David's is perhaps the most dramatic story to emerge from those early days. But the growth and joy we see in all of the Ranchers is not diminished by his successes. All of us at Rainbow Acres work together, and each success one of us has is a victory for all.

21

Everything seemed to be going so well at Rainbow Acres. All of our aspirations seemed to be coming to fruition. But there was something wrong. We had tried to build a residential community, not unlike the residential communities in the normal world. People lived in houses of their own, with families and responsibilities, work to do, money to earn, and as much self-sufficiency as possible. But something was missing—women.

This was a ranch for mentally retarded adult men; that was the problem. The problem reflected itself in sloppy living habits, an abundance of laziness, and a deteriorating social attitude. Perhaps a home for women would provide the missing impetus for the men to develop socially.

All of our planning and all of our thinking had been for a ranch for mentally retarded men. The thought of having women around terrified us. None of us had any experience in institutional programming or intersexual socialization skills or any of that kind of thing. We were set up to house and love people. What kind of drastic changes would we have to make? How would we make this transition?

As we began discussing this with friends and outsiders, the most frequently asked questions seemed to revolve around how many babies we expected the first year. What a thought. One pregnancy, one overt sexual occurrence, would surely close us down. We had intentionally gone very public, for we had wanted everybody to see what we were trying to do. Many eyes were on us; adding women would double the scrutiny from the outside.

We finally decided the advantages of including women in our program outweighed the disadvantages. We also decided to maintain our open-door policy, so often abandoned or avoided by mental retardation facilities. We agreed on these things after long, supportive discussion with the parents and families of our Ranchers. Certainly the most vocal and most supportive of them was Mrs. Yeatman, Ronnie's mother.

Jean Yeatman had made it clear almost from the beginning that she wanted Ronnie in as normal an environment as possible. This included normal socialization and that meant women. When we told her we were considering adding the women's house, she gave her support. "Don't pull back. This is the right move," she said. She probably had as much to do with my final decision as anybody, but that was appropriate, because she and Grant Yeatman had as much to do with defining the purpose of Rainbow Acres as anyone.

During this time our own personal house was being built on some property that I had purchased adjoining the ranch. It was designed to serve as the rest home for the ranch as time and need arose. Its formal Mexican architecture with sun roofs and walls, encircled with Spanish tile drainspouts, gave it an imposing look. As it was nearing completion, we drove up the long graveled driveway to be met by playful workmen pointing brooms and hoe handles through the spouts.

"Halt, who goes there?" mocked a beaming builder.

"What are you doing?" I laughed back.

"You are entering Fort Showers!" came the response.

A sign was hung from twisted tree gateposts, christening this house as Fort Showers for all time. Periodically someone would steal the sign and then days or weeks later it would be mysteriously replaced.

Again, timing was exact. The Showerses moved into their fortress, the Goehners moved into our double wide, and a fourth house was completed for ranchers. All this took place just as we were ready to admit women. In they came, and Rainbow Acres was complete. Two more mobile homes would be added later to bring our capacity up to thirty-two Ranchers, but the general operation was set.

At first, there had been no inquiries from parents of retarded women about the ranch. As time passed, however, more and more parents began looking to us for their children, and we soon had a waiting list of potential female residents. We came to our decision about the time that the requests had grown larger for women than men. So in came the ladies.

Judy, Betty, Gloria, and Linda entered the ranch like the sun in the spring of the last year of life. All of a sudden there was action. Excitement cleansed the air. The men started cleaning up, and the ranch soon took on a very different aspect from the rough, earthy, desert campground it had been. The change seemed to happen overnight.

And babies? We have had one close call that was dealt with firmly, but in a loving way. The men have always treated the women with friendly respect, and the women have given the men polite flattery and a whale of a male ego boost all around. All work equally, all share chores around the ranch, and all participate in ranch activities, sports, and recreation. Our fears had been real, but unfounded. We had fallen into the easy trap of thinking the retarded would be somehow different from society beyond the ranch. We were wrong and are glad to admit it.

Now all we had to do was convince the surrounding community.

So many of the townspeople around the Verde Valley had been supportive. We had received warmth and love from scores of locals. But many still looked at us as strange, perhaps even threatening. Now, with the inclusion of the women, their suspicions doubled. We had to find a way to get through their fears, but how?

I felt an obligation to them, not so much for them to know us, but for us to know them and to try to appeal to them. This was their valley first. They hadn't asked us to come; we had simply appeared.

Then we learned about the Fort Verde Day Parade. It was an annual affair complete with bands and floats. It was made to order—we would enter a float. The whole Verde Valley would see us as a group in that parade.

The parade theme was Camp Verde: Past, Present, and Future. With this in mind we hooked the hay wagon to the pickup and grabbed the crepe paper. We would represent Camp Verde's past with an old-time schoolhouse. The fire bell was lifted off its post and pressed into service atop the "school." The Ranchers dressed themselves to the hilt in old-style western gear. The float was wonderful at a grand total cost of under thirty dollars. Bimbo would lead Alice, the ranch mule, behind the wagon, and we would be a sure hit with the town. What better way to let our neighbors know we cared about the community?

Off we went. The parade started at the white bridge and was to rumble the entire length of the town. The streets were lined with people. I drove the truck and Larry rode in the bed. Ranchers were scattered all over the truck and float while Bimbo and Alice brought up the rear.

Instant pandemonium. Great guffawing laughs came from all sides. Inside the pickup cab my heart stopped. We had blown it. Our gesture was ridiculous. I was so embarrassed and so trapped. All that was left was to fake a grin, wave my hook, and hope to get through them as fast as possible.

What I didn't know was what was going on behind me. Not on the float, but in back with Bimbo and Alice.

Alice, as I have said, was a mule. As such she was doing

her mule thing; that is, she wasn't doing anything. She wouldn't move.

Bimbo was a small mountain of joyous energy. He got behind and pushed. He ran around and pulled. He jumped on and pumped. All to the thrill of the crowd. Bimbo heard them laughing and clapping.

The only thing that man needed was encouragement. No rodeo clown ever performed so well. No mule was ever propelled so hilariously. Bimbo did everything but carry that critter through town. Pushing, prodding, cavorting, and generally doing whatever got the biggest laugh, including teaching the beast how to walk, Bimbo was the hit of the day.

We won first prize for our float, and a major chunk of Camp Verde's heart that day. We weren't home free, but it sure felt good. Home free would come later.

I was at Camp Verde High School's gym one night many weeks later, watching my son play with the school team. The principal came up into the bleachers to see me and ask about the ranch. The school had been very supportive of us.

I told him that I had a dream that someday the Ranchers would be able to attend schools away from Rainbow Acres. I hoped that they would be able to take special classes geared for their learning level, but set up on a more formal educational situation.

He got excited.

So did I. "Boy! Could you pull that off?"

"Give me a couple of days." Up he stood and down the bleachers he went. He was going to give this thing his full effort, and he wasn't waiting around to get started.

The following Monday he phoned to say it was all set. When could we come to sign the Ranchers up? How about right now?

The first class was to be a physical education program. It was to be from eight to nine on Friday evenings. The

Ranchers were to be able to use the high school gym for basketball and we were thrilled.

Something went wrong. The girls' basketball team was scheduled to use the gym at the same time. It was an important game for the high school. Would we mind waiting until after it was over before taking the court?

Never being prone to looking gift horses in the mouth, we agreed to wait until after the game.

We were set up and ready to play when the appointed time came. All suited up in shorts and shirts with "Rainbow Acres" emblazoned upon the backs. The girls' team game ran over its time. It would be very late by the time we could start, so would we hurry on as soon as the game ended? Of course! There would probably still be a lot of spectators in the bleachers, but they should clear out pretty fast, as it was getting late.

Spectators? In fact the gym was packed to standing room only. Most of the Verde Valley had crowded in to see this cross-valley rivalry. All we could do was hope the masses wouldn't walk across the court as they left.

The big game ended. The whistle was blown and the girls hurried off the floor. The instructor said, "Okay, get on out there. We only have forty-five minutes." Out we ran.

The spectators, enroute to the exits, froze in their places.

Stewie, one of the newest Ranchers, was the first on the court. An agile and athletic Down's syndrome victim, he dribbled like a Harlem Globetrotter. Cross-handed, between his legs, the ball went up one hand and across his shoulder to the other hand and down the court for a perfect lay-up. The audience gasped.

David Van Dyken came close behind. An elongated windmill that somehow seemed to keep contact with the ball, David crossed the center line and heaved the ball for a rim-ringing basket. The audience went wild.

Now there were Ranchers all over the place. Betty, one of the first ranch women, was especially adroit, moving like a pro with her small round body. The crowd came unglued.

Those spectators who had left must have heard the cheering and applause, because, by the time I got onto the court, the bleachers were again packed to capacity. Not one single seat emptied during our entire time on the courts. When we finished and began to exit, there came the greatest cheer ever to fill that huge gymnasium—a spontaneous roar of love and approval that echoes to this day throughout the Arizona desert valley.

Articles appeared in valley newspapers and letters poured in. We were welcome to their valley. "How can we help?" the letters asked. "Can we send anything?"

Now we were loved, but still we were not quite home free.

Shortly after the Ranchers' foray into basketball diplomacy, the rains came and brought a major flood to Verde Valley, our green valley. (In Spanish the word *verde* means green, and we were the greenest valley around even though this does seem a bit of a misnomer for a high desert region of sand and rock.) The valley was especially green after our very occasional rainstorms. Rainstorms are life's breath to a desert community, but they can also be a curse. The parched soil cannot absorb a lot of water that falls in a short time, and desert rains tend to mean flash flooding.

This time, the valley was inundated. A river of water, unable to penetrate the ground, washed through Camp Verde as the tiny Verde River outgrew its banks. All around us, the townspeople, the farmers, and others in scattered locations were left in an oozy swamp. Our higher land spared us from any damage, but the Ranchers' hearts went out to their less fortunate neighbors.

A troop of our men headed out to help. The Ranchers helped round up lost animals, cleared trash, and dug out roads. They stopped at all the houses in their path to see if they could help ease the strain of the floods. This lasted for one whole day of exhausting labor. Then the Ranchers went home.

A story appeared in the Camp Verde paper the next day, commenting on the beautiful neighborhood spirit that had been so needed and appreciated during the time of most trouble. All through the story, there was mention only of those wonderful Samaritans who had shared their time to help others save their homes and property. Just general names like "good neighbors," "friends," and other similar expressions were used. At the very last line the story said, "We're thankful that Rainbow Acres is our neighbor."

That was good. *Now* we were home free.

22

The third year at Rainbow Acres was the tough one. So many miracles, so many blessings, so much hard work had taken place, and it was paying off. But the road was not as smooth as we had come to expect.

Larry and I had slipped along a rainbow path that seemed so smooth and perfect. Everything seemed to be going our way. All the growth and changes came so quickly that we didn't have a real opportunity to assess the problems that were coming to the surface.

We had some staff members who were not really aware of what we were trying to do. One such houseparent had taken to beating the Ranchers, and had forbidden them to tell of the beatings. We finally found out and the man was dismissed on the spot, but some damage had been done that would take months to undo.

We found we had some Ranchers that were both mentally retarded and emotionally disturbed. Our inexperience didn't allow us to recognize that this mix couldn't work on our ranch. This caused us much suffering and painful learning.

And then there was the problem of the overall ranch philosophy. This was the question that formed a wedge between Larry and me.

We had always wanted the same things. We wanted a strong and loving home for mentally retarded adults, where a sense of self-sufficiency and independent growth could flourish. Larry, as ranch director, thought we should earn our keep as an agricultural enterprise. We could grow what we needed and sell the rest for income.

I looked around our ten acres of hills and mobile homes and could not see space enough, growable land enough, to keep the ranch fed, let alone provide money crops. It was my belief that the ranch must develop an industrial program to help defray the rising costs and provide Rancher salaries. The land could only provide assistance as an on-site food source. Larry felt the industrial program idea was demeaning to the Ranchers.

Larry objected to many of my fund-raising tactics. I was always off at religious and fraternal organizations, telling my story and the story of the ranch in exchange for a fee and hoped-for follow-up contributions. I was not sure I didn't agree that this was a little demeaning, but I didn't know any other way to bring in the necessary capital.

My accident money was running out. As practicalities started to become more obvious to me, some of the utopian spirit gave way to mundane realities. Larry and I were in total disagreement about how these realities had to be met. One of us was going to have to leave if the ranch was to survive. Because our priorities were different and our assessments of the future were in conflict, the ranch was being torn apart by two loving parents. This had to stop.

Larry and I left the ranch together. We would check into a motel room for as many days as were required and work this out.

"Larry," I said, "I am ready to leave."

"Ralph—" my dear friend started to protest.

"Now, look, I have some money, and I own a house. Things are pretty well set for Marilyn and me." These were painful words, but true. I was best able to handle the move. "I have been thinking of going into politics. Things will be all right. You need the job and I know how much you love the ranch. It's the best way."

"Ralph, no!" Larry's voice was filled with sorrow and

love. "This is your dream. It's the work you were meant to do. You gave your arms—almost your life—for the ranch. I'm the one who has to leave. It's your ranch."

It was a very emotional, very loving two days. Neither of us wanted to leave, but both of us were willing to go for the benefit of the ranch. There was no ego or pride involved, just a loving evaluation of what had to be. Larry was right. For reasons of public knowledge and continuity, it was for me to stay and for the Goehners to go.

I love this man. He is my brother and my son. His muscle and heart made Rainbow Acres live. His sweat and soul made the ranch a real thing. I was losing him not as a friend but as a partner. Larry, Joy, and the kids would head back to the Pacific Northwest, to Washington, to try and start a similar ranch based on agriculture. In a fertile mountain valley, he would set up shop and soon be ready to open another haven for those forgotten handicapped he loves so much.

Now, a new director had to be found for Rainbow Acres. I was determined that Larry's successor be as loving and creative a person as my dear friend. Unlike before, however, we now had a board of directors with some very specific plans of their own. They wanted a professional; education was a prime consideration for them.

This is a sore subject for me. I did very poorly in school. I got through, but barely. Everyone I saw who had a doctorate in this, or a few Master's degrees in that, seemed to be in another world. Most of them didn't really appear to know what was going on in the real world, beyond the idealism of printed pages.

The word went out that a new director was being sought at Rainbow Acres. The response came back, "What must the applicant have? What credentials are you looking for?" I didn't want credentials; I wanted a hard-working, huge-hearted person with skills in a variety of fields. I wanted the new director to get his knowledge here, at the ranch, rather than out of a book.

I had hired many degreed people onto the staff, but very rarely were these people degreed in the areas we were placing them in. I did not want academics or scholars. I wanted to throw out all that fol-de-rol. It's easier to take a person with heart and talent and educate him to a needed skill than to try and replace the talent and love that is so often lost under normal scholastic processing.

I was asked once to speak to the University of Arizona about working with the mentally retarded as a career. I said that I thought it suited most students fine, as they had mostly been retarded by all their years in college. I said quite directly that I didn't believe anybody in the institutional setting was teaching anyone anything about retardation.

The head of the retardation program jumped to his feet and blew his stack.

"Well, what do you want us to do?" he shouted across the auditorium.

"Send them out into the world for a while. I'll tell you exactly what you are doing with your people." This was my subject and I was more than pleased to have the opportunity to vent my frustrations on this group. "You send your students to a state mental institution for a day or so. Then you give them a test that they turn in about six weeks later, and everybody is so proud of what has been done, but your students know less than nothing about mental retardation."

I tend to get very hot about this subject. "All you've done is play the academic game."

My questioner was a bit taken aback at my outburst. "Well, what do you want us to do?"

"Put them in a house with mentally retarded. Let them learn to change bed pans and wet sheets. Let them learn what it is to cook, to be patient, to live with frustration. Then if you want to send them to school, that's fine with me. But first let them know who the retarded are." I was wound up and charging.

"Don't tell your students who retarded people are, because you won't be telling them the truth. For you, the mentally retarded seem to be pigeonholed as numbers. Like those with IQs of 75 to 85 are educable, those 35 to 75 are trainable and those below 35 are severely retarded. That's all useless theory that blocks the minds of your students from really understanding. They have to see for themselves that all handicapped people, including the retarded, are different one from another. They are special, just as each of you is special. Stop blueprinting them and systematizing them. Treat them like people. Love them and they will respond. Analyze them and program them and all you will have will be permanent guinea pigs for your research papers."

This was not about to happen at Rainbow Acres. This was one place where people would grow, not be grown. My new director had to understand that. My board of directors had to understand that.

I had a speaking engagement in Los Angeles around that time. One of the members of my audience was a man named Terry Markham. He and his son Jeff came by to see me after the talk. He was head of Southeast Association Sheltered Workshop in Downey, California, and had been encouraged by my talk. I liked him, particularly the way he handled himself and the way he talked about his own program and young people.

A few phone calls to mutual friends made me like this man Terry even more. I'm kind of sneaky, though, when it comes to learning about people. I like to do a little snooping around to see what mysteries lurk between their words and actions. I went down to Downey to see his operation. I didn't tell him I was coming.

There were around two hundred mentally retarded adults in that workshop. The conditions were good; the workers seemed happy and involved in what they were doing. This was not a sweat shop capitalizing on cheap labor, but a productive place where workers felt important. I was impressed, but it seemed too good to be true.

On several other occasions I went back to California for

speaking stops, and every time I would poke my head in at Downey. It was always the same. Terry and his staff had an excellent working relationship with the retarded. It was a loving environment with strong peripheral and outside programs. Terry Markham was the man I wanted.

Now I had to see if he wanted us. All this time and research could have been in vain, because Terry had no idea that I was looking at him as a possible candidate for a job. Would he even be interested?

Yes, but did I know he had no degrees whatsoever?

There it was. How was I going to get this gifted man past the board? All that skill, all that love and energy and no piece of paper to frame and hang on the wall. I asked him to fill out an application.

My board had decided to hire a high-powered consultant to put together a list of criteria upon which to choose the new director. This man would go through all the applications, examine the candidates, and recommend the perfect choice. I would recommend Terry Markham. The board would have the last say. I was very upset about the whole idea.

Nine applications came in. Five were doctors, two had master's degrees, and one had twenty-five years of experience. Terry had a high school diploma and a lot to offer. The consultant put the applicants through a whole series of tests and interviews, mixed in a large helping of ratios and statistical whatnots, stirred once, and reported that he had a recommendation. One man blew all the other applicants away. I was ready for a fight.

The consultant recommended Terry. All the others had spent so much time in academics and administration that none could touch Terry's actual experience. I gave a skeptical point to the favor of researchers and thanked God for His kindness. Everybody won. The board got its perfect selection, I got my perfect choice, and the ranch got Terry Markham, a perfect director.

Terry's wife, Linda, didn't want to come. The children were about fifty-fifty against it. What now?

But they came. Linda came on staff as my secretary and soon was transformed into a believer. The children fell in love with the spacious beauty of Arizona and all its possibilities. The Markhams were made for Rainbow Acres, and we were just what they needed.

Timing again was the factor. God's wonderful sense of order and need was again proven perfect. Larry was ready to leave; though neither of us knew it, God had need of another home. Terry was ready to move, to expand his horizons, and God had put us together. From all bad there seems to emerge a better good. All the pain and sorrow that had gone on before only seemed to prepare us to appreciate the goodness that was with us now.

But, even then, all obstacles had not been hurdled. I assume they never will be. We still had to compete with my longest, strongest, and most unforgiving antagonist—the government.

23

All my life I have been in combat with the structured system. Throughout my school years I had wanted to dream of the future while the system had wanted me to memorize dates from the past. My pastorates, for the most part, wanted full coffers and full pews while I wanted full hearts and full pews. The government wanted licenses and water systems when they had no license to give and little water to spare.

I had taken a dear friend of mine, whom I will call Mrs. Agnes Bowers, to the Social Security office to help her collect her rightful payments upon the death of her husband. She was a proud upper-middle-class woman who thought of receiving Social Security payments as being on welfare. It took a lot of talking to convince her that (a) the money was rightfully hers, and (b) she would not be made embarrassed by going to sign up for it. She consented to go, but with great fear of humiliation.

I took her to the Social Security office, a rundown suite of rooms covered in faded green paint, hung with instructional signs. Many others sat around the waiting area for their turn—for their plastic number card's turn—to go to the desk.

"Bowers," came the harsh order. "Bowers to the desk."

The room was quiet. Nobody responded. My friend was petrified, horrified. She sat motionless.

"Bowers." The word was like an order.

I stood and moved to the desk.

"Who are you paging, please?" I asked.

"Bowers, A. Bowers," the clerk said gruffly.

"Perhaps if you lowered your voice and requested Mrs. Agnes Bowers, like it says on the form, she would come up to talk with you. These people are not here to serve you. You work for them. Mrs. Bowers pays your salary. Think of her as your boss and call again." My hooks sparkled in the fluorescent light as I gestured to reveal the room of startled citizens. I was very angry and this person knew it.

"Uh-hem—Mrs. Agnes Bowers, please."

"Thank you," I said and went to help my friend to the desk.

I have no tolerance for bureaucrats who have lost sight of who they work for—bureaucrats who by their very nature forget that we are people out here, not just names and numbers.

Such is true of the story about Georgia. She was one of our later women Ranchers. Georgia's family was far from well off. In an attempt to help her, while she was young she had been allowed to work outside an institution and had lived in regular society. It didn't work. She was not ready for that kind of responsibility, so she moved back home. The Social Security people refused her aid because she was supposedly capable of living in normal society, which is a joke.

Georgia is one of the ranch's most socially skillful people. She cares for herself well in a safe environment, but she is still not ready to be thrust penniless onto the streets. We hope she will be able to make continued growing adjustments, as she has made great strides at the ranch. But she is years, if not a lifetime, away from complete self-sufficiency.

An example of Georgia's development came after she had been at the ranch some months. Many people send us old tattered clothes as gifts to the Ranchers. They do this in kindness, but I wonder why they believe the Ranchers would want to wear things so badly mutilated that the original owners have discarded them. Georgia certainly didn't. She took a huge bag of this refuse and ripped it into long shreds. Then, using a loom donated long before she came, she began weaving the scraps into rugs and wall hangings to sell. With the money she made, she told us, she would buy her own clothes. She did just that. Soon she had learned to weave so well that an art store in Sedona hired her part-time to weave for them.

She had come to us broke and friendless. She is now well on her way to self-sufficiency. Given adequate aid from the government, rather than the punishing removal of her rightful benefits, she might have attained this status years earlier.

The government seems to have a skill at taking good programs and either closing them down or making them inoperable. With this knowledge, Larry and I had relied very little on government aid. Terry, on the other hand, recognized our need for even the limited funds we received from the government and argued not to stop them.

Throughout the country a big push toward deinstitutionalization began having an effect. It was obvious that when all those people previously cared for by institutions were turned loose, they would have to be placed somewhere. The government was going to start appointing patients to beds no matter how these people fit into existing programs.

A man from northern Arizona came to meet with Terry and me one day not long after Terry arrived. It was for this very purpose. Rather than beat around the bush, I asked him straight out, "What kind of designs do you have on Rainbow Acres?"

"Seven beds. You owe us seven beds, because we are giving you $13,000 per year."

We had a total budget at Rainbow Acres of $300,000 and seven full mobile homes. We had no room for more bodies without giving up our program. Besides, seven beds now would surely mean three more down the road and maybe a half dozen later. In their attempt to deinstitutionalize they were going to turn us into an institution.

"Do you hear this, Terry? Do you understand what is going to happen?" Terry was new with us. This was a side of him I was not familiar with. "What do you want to do?"

The government man had left. Terry and I walked all over the ranch. All that government money was only a small part of our budget, but the loss of it would cut deeply into our ability to operate.

"Government funding can be pulled away at any time," Terry said slowly. "The administration can change, priorities can change, anything can change, and a program that depends on government funds is out of business."

I should never have worried.

"Besides," I added, "the government is getting more and more belligerent about religious organizations. Even though we aren't a religious group per se, I'm a minister and we do encourage prayer and things."

"Let's get rid of it." The decision was made by the man hired to make it. We were different people, but we thought a lot alike. "It's almost budget time. Let's just get rid of all of it."

Without government funds, we would now have to rely on donations and profits from the industrial center to make our way. We were no longer going to live off the government, but we were certainly not going to die of it either.

So now we were alone. The education establishment had left us (although, surprisingly, was starting to be interested again). The religious world was behind us in spirit, but not in active support. We had intentionally avoided that conflict. Now the government was out. We had talked about self-sufficiency and had it as our goal, but now we had to work on it for our life's blood.

Our industrial center was a mishmash of different projects, mostly handicrafts like weaving pot holders and threading button necklaces. We did some découpage wall plaques over pine slabs with colorful pictures, and we made

greeting cards. None of this was enough to grow on,
however.

Again a story appeared in a newspaper. Rainbow Acres
was going to try to go without government support or
funds. The response, as always, was marvelous. New projects sprang up. Would we sell rainbow candles? Yes!
Would we make and package little rock toys with glued-on
eyes? Yes! How about making leather key chains? You bet!

Rainbow Acres would survive. The money was still
scarce, but sufficient. As I have said, I have what I call a
paranoid faith in God's plan for me and the ranch. Just
when He has given us help to solve a problem, there seems
to be a newer, larger difficulty in its place. Then as we ask
God's help again, and receive it, we are stretched to grow
even more. He has never given us all we want, but He has
always provided what we need, when we need it. That in-
cludes making us have to fight for what we want and need.

All the Ranchers are paid regularly for their work,
whether it is for work in the industrial center, work about
the ranch, or going to high school full time as one of our
young women is now doing. Every other week we have
payday. Every other week the Ranchers go into town to
deposit their money, buy whatever clothes, necessities, or
fun things they want, and feel a part of the community that
has welcomed them so warmly.

One day during our regular bank run, an office worker
at the bank pulled me aside.

"Reverend Showers, we need your help." She was very
professional.

"That's fine; what can I do for you?" I was pleased to try
to be of help.

"Would you sign a piece of paper that allows us to not
hold more than one hundred dollars per Rancher at the
bank."

"Please say that again." I was sure I had misunderstood.

"I would like to have a letter from you simply telling us
that you don't want your people saving more than one hundred dollars each at the bank."

I had heard right.

"Why?" I was feeling the heat build under my collar, but I had to hear her out. Maybe I wasn't understanding.

"Well, we've got a problem with signatures and things like that. Anybody could come in and give a signature and we could never tell if it was authentic, don't you see. Then they could take all the money."

I was madder than spit. I knew very well that wasn't the reason. I knew that they really didn't want the Ranchers in there; they didn't want those strange people in their bank. I couldn't be sure, of course, but that's what I believed I was hearing and it made me furious.

I excused myself as calmly as I could and drove my family, my Ranchers, back home.

I sat and stewed over that woman's words for two days. Then the bank contacted me again. Would I please send the letter they had requested?

No more nice-man junk. I was boiling.

I phoned my attorney, "Can they do that?"

I phoned the bank manager, "You can't do that!"

Then I phoned the main office in Phoenix, "Let me tell you what I'm going to do if you try that!"

I had always received assistance and love from the press. I fully intended to use that friendship to protect my ranch.

"Let's make this very clear," I said to the vice president of the bank. "Unless you get whatever's going on up here at the Camp Verde branch straightened out right now and have them send me an apology and get back to being bankers, I will talk to every reporter in Arizona, California, and New York."

Of course, the people in the home office had no idea of what was going on in this branch office. They did, however, have a very good idea what this kind of press could do to their offices statewide. They also believed that I just might do exactly what I said I would do.

Within three days I received a letter from the manager of the branch bank. This had gotten out of hand; there must have been a mistake; we apologize for any trouble or ill feelings we may have caused you. I received a similar letter from the big boys in Phoenix with a similar apology.

The next time we went into that bank we were met like visiting royalty. They couldn't have been more cordial if I had threatened them with a lawsuit. Over the next while, things sort of evened out and the bank has become one of our biggest supporters. No hard feelings exist on either side and a mutual friendship has developed. All it took was making sure that everybody knew that we would not be discriminated against.

Time passed; the major battles were fought and won. The ranch settled into a successful entity. People thought of us as long-timers, regular members of the community. The press remained our friend.

There we were, a little ranch community, existing in harmony, but no longer making the strong push ahead. We had what we needed, but could lose it to apathy and complacency. There were other organizations trying to get started, but no fire to ignite them. It seemed a shame, but, after all, what more could we ask for? We had all we needed.

24

At Rainbow Acres, miracles keep happening.

I remember a day, when the ranch was still a dream. I had walked to the highest spot on our acreage. There was little there except the unique beauty of the Arizona land. I turned, slowly, in a full 360 degree circle, taking pictures in my mind's eye. "Oh, God," I said, "how much we can do . . . with nothing."

And we had. We had won. We had won over the doubters in the mental-health field. We had bested government red tape. We had challenged the bankers and emerged with the right to live our own lives. It was like a serial, an old-fashioned cliff-hanger, but it was real and true.

Honestly, as I thought about it, we were like early American pioneers; roughing it, dreaming dreams that no one else had, daring to do things that no one else would. Through the love of all our people we had become a community, a community of families.

And what of the Showers family?

Mark has grown up to be a star athlete, when he is not helping me coach Michael's Little League team. Scott has become the intermediary in the family disputes, his calm approach and thoughtfulness never ceasing to amaze me. Michael, who witnessed his father's accident and agony, seems to have left those memories on Pecan Lane, or somewhere. He still has that innocence and enthusiasm—may he never lose them. And Marilyn? She is still the center of everything, the untold, earthbound author of many of the miracles of Rainbow Acres.

Recently, Scott pointed out that he thought we were a closer family since the accident. We seem to spend more time together, sharing more things, being more loving. He cited as an example, oddly, the story of the paddle.

With considerable biblical justification, I am not a believer in sparing the rod when one of the kids is especially awful. I had made a paddle when they were younger and had used it on several occasions. The paddle has gone untouched for several years now, and the boys are nearly men.

They still love to watch me eat, spill, or stab. The other day, Scott watched me chase a soft drink can all over the kitchen floor, trying to hook it, all the while shaking its contents into a foaming frenzy. The spectacle, he said, was too good to miss. I had always said to let me work out my problems, but was this what I wanted? Yes, I am handicapped, but I'm not helpless—pop-top cans or not.

We have thirty Ranchers now, and twenty-two staff members and house-parents. Some Ranchers have come and gone, for various reasons, but most are at home here and happy. Staff turnovers have occurred, but invariably they have been the best for all concerned.

Whenever I become content, or to put it more aptly, too satisfied, I must always ask, "What now, God? What is our next step?"

Occasionally a local paper would print a story about us. Very occasionally it would be a complete retrospective that told the whole story. In April of 1979 one such story appeared in the Scottsdale papers.

A Hollywood film producer, vacationing with his family in Arizona, happened to pick up that Scottsdale newspaper while waiting in a gas station. John Frederick was vice president of FMS, one of the country's most important alcohol and drug-education film companies, but had never even considered doing a film on retardation. He found the article and read it over and over on his way back to California.

Something about the story grabbed him. It was not really his kind of film, but he felt he had to make it.

There followed several phone calls and much excitement. Before he had even met me personally, a director and audio crew came to the ranch to interview Terry, me, and many of the ranchers. Within a month a full film crew was sent out to record and film Rainbow Acres as a thirty-minute educational film for schools and public information programs. They didn't want to stage anything. It was to be an accurate documentary of life at the ranch. Wherever there were Ranchers, there was a camera.

It was John's purpose to make a film that showed the positive lifestyle available to mentally retarded adults, not the more commonly filmed pictures of drooling people and unhappiness. He wanted the retarded world and everyone else to know that life is beautiful, that life can be lived through any adversity in a loving, joyous way. This man truly understood what we were all about. John Frederick was a godsend.

The film received instant acclaim in film festivals, contests, and literary reviews. The phones at Rainbow Acres have never been silent, but now they were beginning to ring off the wall. "Can you help us? We want to start a program like yours for the retarded adults in our area." Rainbow Acres had what it needed, and now we were able to share. God's plan for us was far from complete.

John Frederick was one of so many miracles that God had presented. But the miracles go on. And life goes on. There were times that looked so bleak, times when everything seemed to be going wrong, but God always smiled upon us and life has grown daily more beautiful.

We have the possibility of starting a new ranch for growing our food, and we dream about the new "Sunburst Farm."

I remember a day when I walked with my troubles in the lonely desert behind and beyond the ranch. There was great conflict within me.

I came upon a small hill. All around me was the incredible beauty of Arizona at dawn. The ring of morning dark mountains held the valley in protective silence. Scrub and brush moved in a still-cool breeze, as the gentle sounds of crickets hushed before my step. The muffled sound of sand and stones beneath my boots gave dimension to the sleeping landscape.

I screamed, I cried, I picked up stones and tossed them with all my strength. I kicked the earth and cried out, letting my pain rush out of me.

And then it was done. All the discouragement of the past seemed a far, peaceful distance away. My mind was clear. My heart was calm. I looked about me into the bright day ahead, and saw the loving gifts that God had offered me. I prayed a long, silent prayer of thanks for the gifts and for this moment of relief from struggle.

I knew at that second that all would be well. I looked beyond the road of my future and saw the ranch, thriving in my absence. I saw the whole expanse of what was to be. The ranch area active with staff and Ranchers, the retirement center, the rest home for those who had lived to grow old and now were prepared to die gracefully on this sacred ground. I saw the school, a place where people from all over the world could come to learn of the joy of working with retarded adults and from which they would return to their own worlds, beauty in every soul.

I saw a similar ranch home for the married adult retarded, separated from this ranch, but available to these Ranchers, should time or need arrive. What I did not see was a chain of Rainbow Acres ranches dotted across the country like fast-food restaurants. If there were to be other ranches, others would have to build those needed homes. We would help if asked, but our hearts and efforts would remain here in the Verde Valley.

Rainbow Acres would live. The Ranchers would live. I would live. My mind slipped back to a half-forgotten memory—the day I knew that I would be all right.

I had just left the hospital, my heart still troubled by the fear of not being able to be loved for myself now that I was an unlovely, a handicapped person. My brother-in-law John Walling, his wife Mary-Lou, and daughters Kim and Kristen had come to visit the then-barren ranch. We walked up into the desert, to the place I now stood.

All around was the laughter and frolic of my children and John's two daughters. John tossed a stone into the scrub and said he heard a snake. He did this repeatedly. The small ones yelped and jumped in mock terror. It was a happy time.

As we headed back for home, I walked beside Michael. We talked about unimportant things and enjoyed each other. I did not notice that he had slowed his pace so that the others were far in front of us.

The day had grown dark, the last glow of sunset faded to reveal the stars.

Michael walked in front of me and stopped in my path. His hands reached out and clasped and held my hooks. Gently, he pulled me down to his eye level and whispered to me.

"Daddy, I'm glad God didn't take you, cause I need you." Then he was still, a smile on his face.

Suddenly, all was well. I was needed. I was loved.

For all of us in this world, there is a purpose. None of us is less valuable than the others. Value just takes a different form. We are all God's children. We are all special.

At that instant I understood so much, and yet the message was simple. God doesn't make junk. He makes rainbows.